Better Homes and Gardens®

FIX IT FAST
COOK BOOK

©1979 by Meredith Corporation, Des Moines, Iowa.
All Rights Reserved. Printed in the United States of America.
First Edition. Sixth Printing, 1980.
Library of Congress Catalog Card Number: 78-73180
ISBN: 0-696-00415-1

BETTER HOMES AND GARDENS® BOOKS
Editor: Gerald Knox
Art Director: Ernest Shelton
Associate Art Director: Randall Yontz
Copy and Production Editors: David Kirchner,
    Paul S. Kitzke, David A. Walsh
Fix-It-Fast Cook Book Editors:
    Rosemary C. Hutchinson, Senior Food Editor
    Patricia Teberg, Associate Food Editor
Food Editor: Doris Eby
Senior Associate Food Editor: Sharyl Heiken
Senior Food Editors: Sandra Granseth,
Elizabeth Woolever
Associate Food Editors: Diane Nelson,
Flora Szatkowski, Joy L. Taylor
Recipe Development Editor: Marion Viall
Fix-It-Fast Cook Book Designer: Faith Berven
Senior Graphic Designer: Harijs Priekulis
Graphic Designers: Linda Ford, Richard Lewis,
    Sheryl Veenschoten, Neoma Alt West

CONTENTS

INTRODUCTION

Caught in the what-should-I-fix-for-dinner trap? Whenever you're short on time but still want to prepare appetizing and nutritious foods, turn to the *Fix-It-Fast Cook Book*. Here you'll find a wide selection of speedy recipes that take just 10 to 45 minutes to prepare—and that's from the minute you enter the kitchen until you're putting food on the table.

Start by choosing one of the main dishes, hearty soups, sandwiches, or main-dish salads as the core of your meal. Then round out your menu with recipes from the pages on side-dish salads, vegetables, breads, or desserts. If unexpected company drops by or you decide to throw a party on the spur of the moment, turn to the appetizer section and select one or more snacks or beverages. At the end of the book you'll find a collection of special tips to guide you through the ins and outs of planning and preparing quick meals for all occasions, as well as recipes for timesaving mixes to make ahead and keep on hand.

A plain omelet becomes an elegant dessert when you fill a basic Dessert Omelet, top, with any of six luscious fillings (see recipes, page 76).

Serve a variety of different salads by mixing and matching a Basic Tossed Salad, center, with any of six different dressings (see recipes, page 46).

Toss fettucini, bacon, and parmesan cheese with a rich cream sauce to make company-special Fettucini Carbonara, bottom (see recipe, page 26).

Quick Steak Italiano

35 MINUTES

- 4 beef or pork cubed steaks (1 pound total)
- 1 tablespoon cooking oil
- 4 ounces bulk Italian sausage
- ½ cup chopped onion
- 1 8-ounce can tomato sauce
- ¾ cup apple juice or apple cider
- ½ teaspoon garlic salt
- ½ teaspoon dried oregano, crushed
- 2 tablespoons cornstarch
  Hot buttered noodles

In skillet brown steaks in hot oil; remove from pan. In skillet cook sausage and onion till meat is browned; drain. Add tomato sauce, apple juice, garlic salt, oregano, and ⅛ teaspoon *pepper*. Heat and stir to boiling. Add steaks to skillet. Cover; simmer 10 minutes. Remove meat; keep warm. Mix cornstarch and 2 tablespoons *cold water*; stir into skillet. Cook and stir till bubbly. Toss noodles with dried parsley flakes, if desired. Serve meat with sauce over noodles. Top with grated parmesan cheese, if desired. Serves 4.

Spanish Steak and Rice

40 MINUTES

- 1 6-ounce package *instant* Spanish rice mix
- 1¼ to 1½ pounds beef cubed steaks, cut into ½-inch-wide strips
- 2 tablespoons cooking oil
- 1 medium green pepper, cut into strips
- ¼ cup hot-style catsup
- 1 tablespoon cornstarch
- 1 teaspoon sugar

Prepare rice mix according to package directions. Meanwhile, in large skillet brown *half* the meat at a time in hot oil. Return all meat to pan. Add pepper. In screw-top jar mix catsup, cornstarch, sugar, 1 cup *cold water*, and 1 teaspoon *salt*. Shake to blend; add to skillet. Cook and stir till mixture bubbles. Cook and stir 1 to 2 minutes more. Stir in hot rice; heat through. Serves 6.

Deviled Beef Rolls

25 MINUTES
For easier rolling, trim steaks square–

- 2 tablespoons *regular* onion soup mix
- 3 tablespoons horseradish mustard
- 4 beef cubed steaks (1 pound total)
- 1 4-ounce can sliced mushrooms, drained
- 2 tablespoons butter, melted

Preheat broiler. Meanwhile, mix dry soup mix and 4 teaspoons *water*; let stand 5 minutes. Stir in mustard. Sprinkle steaks with a little pepper. Spread one side of each steak with one-fourth of the mustard mixture; top with one-fourth of the mushrooms. Roll up steaks and fasten with wooden picks. Brush with butter. Broil 4 to 5 inches from heat 6 minutes. Turn, brushing with butter; broil 6 minutes more. Serves 4.

Choose-a-Butter Steak

20 MINUTES

Place ¼ cup *butter* in a heat-proof bowl in cold oven. Turn oven to 350°. Soften butter 3 minutes. Meanwhile, slash fat edge of 2 pounds *beef sirloin steak*, cut 1 inch thick. Remove bowl from oven; transfer butter to cool bowl. (If butter is kept in hot bowl, it will melt rather than soften.) Turn oven to broil. Broil steak 3 inches from heat 12 to 14 minutes for medium, turning once. Season with salt and pepper. Mix butter with *desired seasoning below*. Dollop atop each serving. Serves 4.
Basil: 1 tablespoon *catsup* and ½ teaspoon dried *basil*, crushed.
Blue Cheese: 1 tablespoon crumbled *blue cheese*.
Dill: ¼ teaspoon dried *dillweed*.
Caraway: ½ teaspoon *caraway seed*.
Fennel: ¼ teaspoon *fennel seed*, crushed.

Use either beef or pork cubed steaks to prepare hearty Quick Steak Italiano.

MAIN DISHES

Lima-Beef Stew

45 MINUTES

To prevent the biscuit topper from being doughy, make sure the stew mixture is boiling when you add the topper –

- 1½ pounds beef top round steak, cut into ½-inch cubes
- 2 tablespoons cooking oil
- 1 16-ounce can whole small carrots
- 1 16-ounce can lima beans
- 2 cups frozen small whole onions or 1 15½-ounce can boiled onions, drained
- 1 10¾-ounce can condensed tomato soup
- 2 teaspoons brown sugar
- ½ teaspoon dried thyme, crushed
- 1¼ cups Whole Wheat-Honey Biscuit Mix (see recipe, page 92)
- ⅓ cup milk

In large saucepan or Dutch oven cook beef cubes *half* at a time in hot cooking oil till browned. Return all the meat cubes to pan. Stir in *undrained* carrots, *undrained* lima beans, and frozen or drained canned onions. Stir in tomato soup, brown sugar, and thyme. Bring mixture to boiling. Combine Whole Wheat-Honey Biscuit Mix and milk. Drop batter in 6 mounds atop *boiling* mixture. Cover; simmer 10 minutes. Uncover; simmer 10 minutes more. Serve in soup bowls. Makes 6 servings.

If you have a little extra time, here's an easy way to slice any meat into perfect thin slices. The secret is to partially freeze the meat for 45 to 60 minutes and then slice it across the grain. If you're thawing frozen meat, cut the slices when the meat is still icy.

Curry-Beef Stir-Fry

35 MINUTES

- 1 pound beef top round or flank steak
- 1 tablespoon soy sauce
- 1 medium onion
- 1½ cups beef broth
- 3 tablespoons all-purpose flour
- 2 teaspoons curry powder
- ¾ teaspoon salt
- 3 tablespoons cooking oil
- 3 cups fresh broccoli buds, cut into 1-inch pieces
- Chow mein noodles

Thinly slice beef across the grain into bite-size strips. Place in bowl; sprinkle with soy sauce. Cut onion into thin wedges. Set meat and onion aside. Stir together broth, flour, curry powder, and salt; set aside.

Heat wok or large skillet over high heat; add *2 tablespoons* of the cooking oil. Stir-fry onion and broccoli 4 minutes. Remove vegetables. Add remaining 1 tablespoon oil to wok. Add *half* the meat; stir-fry 2 minutes. Remove meat. Repeat with remaining meat. Push meat away from center of wok. Stir flour-broth mixture; add to center of wok. Cook and stir till bubbly. Return all meat and vegetables to pan. Cover; cook 1 minute more. Serve over chow mein noodles. Serves 6.

Chili

35 MINUTES

For added flavor, top with corn chips –

- 1 pound ground beef
- ½ cup chopped onion
- 1 15½-ounce can red kidney beans
- 1 10-ounce can mild enchilada sauce
- 1 8¾-ounce can whole kernel corn
- ¼ cup water
- ½ teaspoon salt

In a 10-inch skillet cook beef and onion till beef is browned and onion is tender. Drain. Stir in *undrained* beans, enchilada sauce, *undrained* corn, water, and salt. Simmer, covered, 20 minutes. Makes 4 servings.

Beef-Vegetable Stew

40 MINUTES

1 pound ground beef
1 medium onion, thinly sliced and
  separated into rings
1 10¾-ounce can condensed
  golden mushroom soup
½ cup French salad dressing
¼ cup Beef Gravy Base (see recipe,
  page 90) or 1 1-ounce envelope
  brown gravy mix
2 tablespoons vinegar
1 16-ounce can sliced carrots
1 16-ounce can sliced potatoes
1 4-ounce can sliced mushrooms
¾ cup Homemade Biscuit Mix (see
  recipe, page 92) or packaged
  biscuit mix
¼ cup milk

In 4-quart Dutch oven cook beef and onion till beef is browned and onion is tender; drain. Stir in soup, salad dressing, Gravy Base, and vinegar. Stir in *undrained* carrots, potatoes, and mushrooms. Bring to boiling; stir often. Meanwhile, combine Biscuit Mix and milk. Drop batter in 6 dumplings atop *boiling* mixture. Cover; simmer 10 minutes. Uncover. Cook 10 minutes more. Serves 6.

Cranberry Macaroni

25 MINUTES

Cooking the macaroni while you simmer the sauce makes this dish extra speedy –

1 pound ground beef
1 8-ounce can tomato sauce
1 8-ounce can jellied cranberry
  sauce
½ cup water
¼ cup bottled barbecue sauce
½ teaspoon salt
½ teaspoon ground ginger
¼ teaspoon ground cinnamon
  Hot cooked macaroni

In 10-inch skillet brown meat; drain excess fat. Stir in tomato sauce, cranberry sauce, water, barbecue sauce, and seasonings. Cook, uncovered, over medium-low heat 15 to 20 minutes. Serve over hot macaroni. Makes 4 servings.

Speedy Stroganoff

35 MINUTES

1 pound ground beef
¾ cup Beef Gravy Base (see recipe,
  page 90)
1 4-ounce can sliced mushrooms
2 tablespoons catsup
2 tablespoons dry sherry
½ cup sour cream dip with onion
  Hot cooked noodles or rice

In a saucepan brown ground beef; drain. Stir in Beef Gravy Base. Stir in *undrained* mushrooms and catsup. Add 1 cup *water*. Cover; bring to boiling. Simmer, covered, 15 minutes. Stir in wine. Gradually blend 1 cup beef mixture into the sour cream dip. Return to saucepan. Heat through *(do not boil)*. Serve over noodles. Sprinkle with paprika, if desired. Makes 4 servings.

Taco Pizza

40 MINUTES

Using lean meat allows you to skip browning the ground beef –

1 12-inch Frozen Pizza Crust (see
  recipe, page 91) or commercial
  frozen pizza crust
1 8-ounce can tomato sauce
1 tablespoon Mexican Seasoning
  Mix (see recipe, page 90) or
  taco seasoning mix
¾ pound *very lean* ground beef
1 canned green chili pepper,
  rinsed, seeded, and chopped
1½ cups shredded cheddar cheese
  (6 ounces)
1 cup shredded lettuce
1 medium tomato, chopped
¼ cup crumbled corn chips

Preheat oven to 425°. Meanwhile, place Pizza Crust on pizza pan or baking sheet. Mix tomato sauce and Mexican Seasoning. Spread over crust. Dot with beef. Sprinkle with chili pepper and cheese. Bake in 425° oven 20 to 25 minutes or till meat is cooked and cheese is melted. Sprinkle with lettuce, tomato, and corn chips. Serves 4.

MAIN DISHES

Beef-and-Bean Stew

45 MINUTES
Use the beans and carrots undrained –

- 1 pound ground beef
- ½ pound bulk pork sausage
- 2 15-ounce cans great northern beans
- 1 8-ounce can diced carrots
- 1 8-ounce can tomato sauce
- 1 tablespoon minced dried onion
- 1 tablespoon dried green pepper flakes
- 1 tablespoon worcestershire sauce
- 2 teaspoons instant beef bouillon granules
- ½ teaspoon paprika

In large saucepan brown beef and sausage, being careful to leave meat in chunks; drain. Stir in remaining ingredients. Bring to boiling. Cover; simmer 30 minutes. Makes 6 servings.

Polka Dot Meat Cups

45 MINUTES
There's no need to grease the muffin cups for these tasty individual meat loaves –

- 1½ cups frozen loose-pack hash brown potatoes
- 1 beaten egg
- ¾ cup tomato sauce
- ¾ cup soft bread crumbs (1 slice)
- 1 tablespoon Italian Seasoning Mix (see recipe, page 90)
- ¾ teaspoon salt
  Dash pepper
- 1 pound ground beef

Preheat oven to 375°. Meanwhile, spread potatoes on paper toweling; let stand 5 minutes. In large bowl combine egg, ¼ cup of the tomato sauce, bread crumbs, Italian Seasoning, salt, and pepper. Add ground beef; mix well. Fold in hash brown potatoes. Divide into 8 portions; shape into balls. Place one in each of eight 2½-inch muffin pans. Bake in 375° oven for 20 minutes. Top each with some of the remaining tomato sauce. Bake 5 to 10 minutes more. Serves 4.

Green Bean Moussaka

45 MINUTES
This easy casserole has a flavor reminiscent of the classic Greek dish –

- 1 pound ground beef
- 1 tablespoon all-purpose flour
- 1 8-ounce can tomato sauce
- ½ teaspoon garlic salt
- ¼ teaspoon ground cinnamon
- 1 16-ounce can French-style or cut green beans, drained
- 2 slightly beaten eggs
- 1 12-ounce carton (1½ cups) cream-style cottage cheese with chives
- ¼ cup grated parmesan cheese
- 2 tablespoons sliced pitted ripe olives

Preheat oven to 375°. Meanwhile, in medium skillet brown beef; drain fat. Stir in flour. Add tomato sauce, garlic salt, and cinnamon. Place green beans in 10x6x2-inch baking dish. Spread the meat mixture atop. Combine eggs and cottage cheese; spoon over meat mixture. Sprinkle with parmesan cheese. Bake in 375°oven for 25 minutes. Top with olives. Serves 6.

Microwave Method: In nonmetal bowl crumble beef. Cook, covered, in countertop microwave oven on high power for 5 minutes, stirring several times. Drain. Stir in flour. Stir in tomato sauce, garlic salt, and cinnamon. Place green beans in 10x6x2-inch baking dish; top with meat mixture. Combine eggs and cottage cheese; spoon over meat. Sprinkle with parmesan. Micro-cook, covered, 7 to 8 minutes, giving dish a half-turn twice. Top with olives.

Save time by making soft bread crumbs in batches and storing them in the freezer till you need them. Make the crumbs by tearing pieces of bread into quarters. Blend 2 or 3 slices at a time, covered, in a blender (or food processor) to coarse crumbs (1 slice of bread will give ¾ cup crumbs). Freeze in a tightly covered freezer container. To measure the frozen crumbs, stir them with a spoon and press lightly into a measuring cup.

Spicy Chili Mac

35 MINUTES

For a milder flavor, use only 1 tablespoon of the Mexican Seasoning —

  1 pound ground beef
  ¾ cup chopped green pepper
  1 16-ounce can tomatoes, cut up
  1 15½-ounce can red kidney beans
  1 8-ounce can tomato sauce
  2 tablespoons Mexican Seasoning
      Mix (see recipe, page 90)
  1 bay leaf
  1 cup uncooked elbow macaroni

In skillet cook meat and pepper till meat is browned; drain fat. Stir in *undrained* tomatoes, *undrained* kidney beans, tomato sauce, Mexican Seasoning, bay leaf, ½ cup *water*, and 1¼ teaspoons *salt*. Bring to boiling; add macaroni. Cover; simmer, stirring often, 15 to 20 minutes or till macaroni is done. Remove bay leaf. Makes 6 servings.

Mushroom-Beef Patties

25 MINUTES

  1 3-ounce can chopped
      mushrooms
  1 cup herb-seasoned stuffing mix
  1 cup dairy sour cream
  ¼ cup finely chopped onion
  2 teaspoons worcestershire sauce
  ¼ teaspoon ground nutmeg
  1 pound ground beef
  4 1-inch slices French bread
  2 tablespoons dijon-style mustard

Preheat broiler. Meanwhile, drain mushrooms, reserving ¼ cup liquid. Mix ⅓ cup of the mushrooms, the stuffing mix, ⅓ cup sour cream, onion, worcestershire, and nutmeg. Add beef; mix well. Shape into four 5-inch patties. Broil 3 to 4 inches from heat 5 to 6 minutes. Turn; broil 5 to 6 minutes more. Toast bread in broiler pan during last few minutes of broiling. Meanwhile, in saucepan mix the reserved liquid, remaining mushrooms, remaining sour cream, and mustard. Heat through (*do not boil*). Serve patties on bread. Top with sauce. Serves 4.

Burger-Noodle Supper

25 MINUTES

  1 beaten egg
  ¼ cup quick-cooking rolled oats
  1 tablespoon worcestershire sauce
  2 teaspoons minced dried onion
  ¼ teaspoon dry mustard
  ¼ teaspoon instant beef bouillon
      granules
  1 pound ground beef
  ⅔ cup Beef Gravy Base (see recipe,
      page 90) or 1 10¼-ounce can
      beef gravy
      Hot cooked noodles

In mixing bowl mix egg, oats, worcestershire, onion, mustard, bouillon granules, 2 tablespoons *water*, ½ teaspoon *salt*, and ⅛ teaspoon *pepper*. Add beef; mix well. Shape into four 4-inch patties. In large skillet brown patties on both sides, 3 to 4 minutes per side. Mix Gravy Base and 1 cup *water*. Pour over patties. (If using canned gravy, pour *undiluted* gravy over patties.) Bring to boiling; cook and stir 1 minute more. Serve over noodles. Serves 4.

Individual Ham Puffs

45 MINUTES

This dish is pictured on page 13 —

  4 eggs
  ½ cup milk
  ½ teaspoon dry mustard
  ⅛ teaspoon pepper
  4 ounces brick cheese, cut up
  2 3-ounce packages cream cheese,
      cut up
  1 cup finely diced fully cooked
      ham (5 ounces)
  ½ teaspoon dried parsley flakes

Preheat oven to 375°. Meanwhile, in blender container mix eggs, milk, mustard, and pepper. Cover; blend till smooth. With blender running, add cheeses through opening in lid or with lid ajar. Blend till nearly smooth. Stir in ham and parsley. Pour into four *ungreased* 1-cup soufflé dishes. Bake in 375° oven 25 to 30 minutes or till set. Serves 4.

Ham-Vegetable Stew

35 MINUTES

2 tablespoons all-purpose flour
1 tablespoon minced dried onion
1 tablespoon dried green pepper flakes
1 teaspoon instant chicken bouillon granules
¼ teaspoon dried thyme, crushed
1 23-ounce can sweet potatoes, cut up
2½ cups cubed fully cooked ham
1 16-ounce can tomatoes, cut up
1 teaspoon worcestershire sauce
1 cup Homemade Biscuit Mix (see recipe, page 92) or packaged biscuit mix
½ teaspoon dry mustard
¼ cup milk

Preheat oven to 400°. Meanwhile, in saucepan mix first five ingredients, ¼ teaspoon *salt*, and ⅛ teaspoon *pepper*. Stir in potatoes, ham, tomatoes, and worcestershire. Bring to boiling. Mix Biscuit Mix and mustard. Blend in milk. On floured surface pat dough to 5-inch circle; cut into 6 wedges. Turn *hot* ham mixture into 2-quart casserole. Quickly top with biscuit wedges. Bake in 400° oven 18 to 20 minutes. Serves 6.

Applesauce Ham Loaves

40 MINUTES

1 slightly beaten egg
¾ cup soft bread crumbs
1 8½-ounce can applesauce
1½ teaspoons minced dried onion
1 teaspoon dijon-style mustard
1 teaspoon snipped parsley
½ pound bulk pork sausage
½ pound ground fully cooked ham
1 tablespoon brown sugar
1 tablespoon vinegar

Preheat oven to 375°. Mix egg, crumbs, ¼ cup of the applesauce, onion, mustard, parsley, ¼ teaspoon *salt*, and dash *pepper*. Add meats; mix. Shape into 4 loaves. Place in 11x7½x2-inch baking dish. Make hollows in loaves. Mix remaining applesauce, sugar, and vinegar; pour into hollows. Bake in 375° oven 25 minutes. Serves 4.

Omelet with Ham Sauce

45 MINUTES
Make sure beaters are perfectly clean before beating egg whites to ensure getting a high volume –

4 egg yolks
¼ teaspoon salt
4 egg whites
1 tablespoon water
2 tablespoons butter or margarine
2 tablespoons chopped onion
1 tablespoon butter or margarine
1 tablespoon all-purpose flour
  Dash pepper
½ cup milk
⅓ cup shredded American cheese (1½ ounces)
½ teaspoon dried parsley flakes
½ cup diced fully cooked ham
2 tablespoons chopped pimiento

Preheat oven to 325°. Meanwhile, in small mixer bowl beat egg yolks and salt on high speed of electric mixer about 6 minutes or till thickened and lemon-colored. Wash beaters. In large mixer bowl beat egg whites and water till frothy. Beat to stiff peaks. Fold egg yolks into egg whites. In 10-inch oven-going skillet, heat the 2 tablespoons butter over medium-high heat till bubbly. Pour in egg mixture, spreading mixture higher at sides. Reduce heat; cook slowly, about 7 minutes or till puffy and set. Bake in 325° oven for 7 to 8 minutes or till knife inserted just off-center comes out clean.

Meanwhile, prepare sauce in saucepan. Cook onion in 1 tablespoon butter till tender. Blend in flour and pepper; add milk. Cook and stir till bubbly. Add cheese and parsley, stirring till cheese melts. Stir in ham and pimiento; keep warm. To serve, loosen sides of omelet. Make a shallow cut across omelet slightly above center. Spoon *one-third* of sauce over larger portion of omelet. Tilt pan; fold omelet in half. Slide onto serving plate. Serve with remaining ham sauce. Makes 3 or 4 servings.

Both Individual Ham Puffs, front (see recipe, page 11), and Ham-Vegetable Stew, back, are company-special main dishes that are ready in just minutes.

Choose-a-Sauce Chops

40 MINUTES

- 6 pork chops, cut ½ inch thick
- 2 tablespoons cooking oil
  Cran-Orange Sauce or Barbecue Sauce (see recipes below)
- 2 tablespoons cold water
- 1 teaspoon cornstarch

Trim fat from chops; season with a little salt and pepper. In a 12-inch skillet cook chops in hot oil, 10 to 15 minutes or till done, turning once; drain fat. Add desired sauce. Cover; simmer 5 minutes. Remove chops to platter; keep warm. Blend water into cornstarch. Add to sauce in skillet. Cook and stir till bubbly. Spoon some sauce over chops; pass remaining. Serves 6.

Cran-Orange Sauce

5 MINUTES

- 1 8-ounce can whole cranberry sauce
- ⅓ cup orange marmalade
- 2 tablespoons water
- 1 teaspoon instant chicken bouillon granules
- 1 teaspoon lemon juice
- ½ teaspoon ground ginger
  Dash garlic powder

In bowl combine cranberry sauce, marmalade, water, bouillon granules, lemon juice, ginger, and garlic powder. Use with Choose-a-Sauce Chops. Makes about ¾ cup.

Barbecue Sauce

5 MINUTES

- ½ cup catsup
- ¼ cup packed brown sugar
- ¼ cup vinegar
- 2 teaspoons grated onion
- 1 teaspoon dry mustard

In bowl mix catsup, brown sugar, vinegar, onion, and mustard. Use with Choose-a-Sauce Chops. Makes ½ cup.

Pork Pepper Steak

30 MINUTES
Try this stir-fry recipe with beef, too –

- ¾ pound boneless pork
- 1 medium green pepper
- 1 15½-ounce can pineapple chunks
- ¼ cup soy sauce
- 1 tablespoon cornstarch
- 1 tablespoon honey
- ½ teaspoon instant chicken bouillon granules
- 1 clove garlic, minced
- ⅛ teaspoon pepper
- 2 tablespoons cooking oil
  Hot cooked rice

Thinly slice pork into bite-size strips. Cut green pepper into 1-inch squares. Drain pineapple, reserving syrup; add enough water to make ¾ cup liquid. In bowl stir syrup mixture and soy into cornstarch. Stir in honey, bouillon granules, garlic, and pepper. Heat wok or large skillet over high heat; add oil. Stir-fry pork and green pepper in hot oil 3 to 4 minutes or till meat is browned. Push pieces away from center of wok. Stir soy mixture; add to center of wok along with pineapple. Cook and stir till thickened and bubbly. Combine with meat and pepper. Cover; heat 1 minute. Serve over rice. Serves 4.

Sausage-Kraut Pizza

35 MINUTES

- 1 Frozen Pizza Crust (see recipe, page 91) or commercial frozen pizza crust
- 1 8-ounce can tomato sauce
- 1 8-ounce can sauerkraut, drained, and finely snipped
- ½ teaspoon caraway seed
- ½ pound Polish sausage, sliced
- 1½ cups shredded Swiss cheese (6 ounces)

Preheat oven to 425°. Meanwhile, place frozen crust on pizza pan or baking sheet. Spread tomato sauce over crust. Mix sauerkraut and caraway seed. Sprinkle atop pizza. Dot with sausage. Bake in 425° oven 15 minutes. Top with cheese. Bake 5 minutes. Serves 4.

Apple-Sausage Hash

35 MINUTES

¼ cup butter or margarine
2 tablespoons brown sugar
2 medium apples, cored and sliced
¼ cup chopped onion
3 cups frozen loose-pack hash brown potatoes
1 16-ounce can sauerkraut, rinsed and drained
1 12-ounce package Polish sausage, halved crosswise
½ teaspoon poppy seed

In 12-inch skillet melt butter. Add brown sugar. Stir in apples and onion. Cook 3 minutes or till almost tender. Stir in frozen potatoes, sauerkraut, sausage, poppy seed, ½ teaspoon *salt*, and ⅛ teaspoon *pepper*. Simmer, covered, 15 minutes. Stir occasionally. Serves 6.
Microwave Method: Place butter in 2-quart nonmetal casserole. Cook in countertop microwave oven on high power for 1 minute. Stir in sugar. Add apples and onion. Micro-cook, covered, 4 minutes. Stir in potatoes, sauerkraut, sausage, poppy seed, ¼ teaspoon *salt*, and ⅛ teaspoon *pepper*. Micro-cook, covered, 12 minutes, stirring twice.

Smoky Potato Bake

45 MINUTES

1 12-ounce package fully cooked smoked sausage links
1 5½-ounce package dry au gratin potatoes
1 cup chopped celery

Preheat oven to 400°. Meanwhile, halve 3 sausage links crosswise; slice remaining. Prepare potatoes according to package directions *except* omit butter. Stir in celery and sliced sausage. Turn into 1½-quart casserole. Bake in 400° oven 25 minutes. Stir. Place halved links atop. Bake 10 minutes more. Serves 6.
Microwave Method: Fix as above *except* use 3-quart nonmetal casserole. Cook, covered, in countertop microwave oven on high power using microwave directions on potato package. Place link halves atop. Micro-cook, uncovered, 2 minutes.

Skillet Pizza

40 MINUTES
Try this pizza with ground beef, too –

1 15⅝-ounce package cheese pizza mix
1 tablespoon Italian Seasoning Mix (see recipe, page 90)
½ pound bulk pork sausage or Italian sausage
½ cup sliced pitted ripe olives
1½ cups shredded mozzarella cheese (6 ounces)

In a bowl blend flour packet from mix with ½ cup *hot water* to form a soft dough. With greased hands spread dough into a greased cold heavy 10-inch skillet. Press over bottom and ½ inch up sides. Cook over medium-low heat 7 minutes with lid of skillet ajar. Meanwhile, combine sauce from mix and Italian Seasoning. In another skillet brown sausage; drain. Stir in *half* of the sauce mixture. Remove skillet with crust from heat; spread remaining sauce mixture atop. Sprinkle with cheese from mix. Top with sausage mixture and olives. Sprinkle with mozzarella. Cook over medium-low heat with lid ajar 15 minutes more. Uncover; cook 6 to 8 minutes. Loosen sides and bottom of pizza. Slide onto plate. Serves 4.

Franks and Rice

25 MINUTES

½ cup chopped onion
⅓ cup chopped green pepper
2 tablespoons butter
1 16-ounce can tomatoes, cut up
1 15½-ounce can red kidney beans
1 12-ounce package frankfurters, cut into 1-inch pieces
1½ cups quick-cooking rice
¼ cup water
1 teaspoon dried basil, crushed

In large saucepan cook onion and green pepper in butter till tender. Stir in *undrained* tomatoes, *undrained* beans, franks, rice, water, basil, and ½ teaspoon *salt*. Bring to boiling, stirring frequently. Cover; simmer 5 to 7 minutes more. Makes 4 or 5 servings.

MAIN DISHES

Quick Frank Quiche

45 MINUTES

1 package (8) refrigerated crescent rolls
1 3-ounce can French-fried onions
6 ounces frankfurters, sliced
1 cup shredded mozzarella or Swiss cheese (4 ounces)
2 beaten eggs
1 5⅓-ounce can evaporated milk
½ teaspoon dry mustard
½ teaspoon dried parsley flakes

Preheat oven to 350°. Unroll rolls; press 2 rolls onto bottom and sides of each of four 5-inch tart pans (or use 4 rolls in each of two 6½-inch quiche pans). Sprinkle *half* the onion and all the meat among pans. Top with cheese. Mix eggs, milk, mustard, parsley, and ¼ teaspoon *salt*. Pour over cheese. Place pans on baking sheet. Bake in 350° oven 20 minutes. Top with remaining onion during last 5 minutes. Serves 4.

Corn-Frank Supper

40 MINUTES

2 eggs
2 cups Corn Bread Mix (see recipe, page 91) or 1 14-ounce package corn bread mix
1 11-ounce can condensed cheddar cheese soup
12 ounces frankfurters, sliced
⅓ cup sliced pitted ripe olives
2 tablespoons chopped pimiento
1 tablespoon dried parsley flakes
1 teaspoon worcestershire sauce
1 cup dairy sour cream
3 tablespoons all-purpose flour

Preheat oven to 425°. Meanwhile, beat eggs and 1 cup *water* with rotary beater. Add Bread Mix; beat smooth. Pour into greased 9x9x2-inch baking pan. Bake in 425° oven 20 to 25 minutes. (Or, make packaged mix according to package directions.) Heat soup and 1 cup *water* to boiling. Stir in next five ingredients; heat through. Mix sour cream and flour; stir into soup mixture. Cook and stir till bubbly. Serve over bread. Serves 6.

Sweet-Sour Meatballs

30 MINUTES
Use homemade Freezer Meatballs straight from the freezer –

1 20-ounce can pineapple chunks
¾ cup maple-flavored syrup
½ cup vinegar
20 Freezer Meatballs (see recipe, page 91)
1 large green pepper, cut into ¾-inch pieces
½ cup maraschino cherries, drained
2 tablespoons cornstarch
½ teaspoon salt
¼ cup cold water
Hot cooked rice

Drain pineapple, reserving syrup. Set pineapple chunks aside. In saucepan combine reserved pineapple syrup, maple syrup, and vinegar. Add frozen meatballs; bring to boiling. Simmer, covered, 15 minutes or till meatballs are hot. Add drained pineapple, green pepper, and cherries. Stir together cornstarch and salt. Stir in water. Blend into mixture in saucepan. Cook and stir about 5 minutes or till pepper is almost tender. Serve over hot cooked rice. Makes 4 servings.

Microwave Method: In 3-quart non-metal casserole cook meatballs, covered, in countertop microwave oven on high power for 3 minutes or till thawed; rearrange once. Remove meatballs; set aside. In same casserole combine *un-drained* pineapple, maple syrup, vinegar, green pepper, and cherries. Micro-cook, covered, 10 minutes or till bubbly. Stir together cornstarch and salt. Stir in water. Blend into pineapple mixture. Micro-cook 2 minutes more, stirring once. Add meatballs; micro-cook 4 to 5 minutes or till meatballs are hot, stirring once. Serve as above.

Frankfurters, French-fried onions, mozzarella cheese, and evaporated milk give impressive Quick Frank Quiche a rich delicate flavor, while refrigerated crescent rolls make the crust foolproof. To make four quiches, double the recipe.

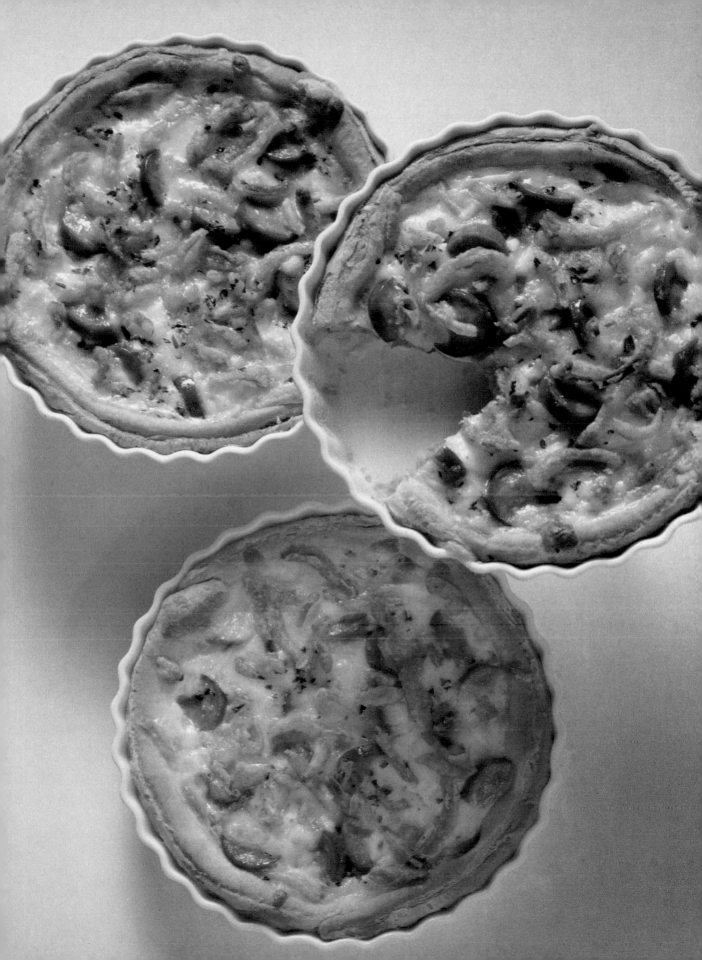

MAIN DISHES

Meatballs Carbonnade

35 MINUTES

- 3 slices bacon
- 2 medium onions, thinly sliced
- ¼ cup all-purpose flour
- 2 teaspoons instant beef bouillon granules
- 2 teaspoons brown sugar
- 2 teaspoons vinegar
- ½ teaspoon salt
- ½ teaspoon dried thyme, crushed
- 1 12-ounce can (1½ cups) beer
- 20 Freezer Meatballs (see recipe, page 91)
- 2 tablespoons snipped parsley

In skillet cook bacon till crisp. Drain bacon, reserving drippings in skillet. Crumble bacon; set aside. In skillet cook onion in drippings till tender. Stir in flour, bouillon granules, brown sugar, vinegar, salt, thyme, and dash pepper. Add beer. Cook and stir till mixture bubbles. Stir in frozen meatballs. Cover; simmer 20 minutes. Top with parsley and bacon. Makes 4 servings.

Fiesta Meatballs

30 MINUTES

Keep a supply of nuts on hand to use whenever you need them. Store the nuts in the freezer to keep them fresher longer –

- 20 Freezer Meatballs (see recipe, page 91)
- 1½ cups chicken broth
- ½ cup bottled spaghetti sauce
- 1 tablespoon dried parsley flakes
- 2 teaspoons minced dried onion
- ¼ teaspoon garlic powder
- ¼ cup slivered almonds
- 1 tablespoon cornstarch
- 1 tablespoon cold water
  Hot cooked rice

In large saucepan combine frozen meatballs, chicken broth, spaghetti sauce, parsley, onion, and garlic powder. Bring to boiling; cover. Simmer 15 to 20 minutes or till meatballs are hot. Stir in nuts. Blend cornstarch and water; stir into meat mixture. Cook and stir till bubbly. Serve over rice. Serves 4.

Onion-Meatball Supper

30 MINUTES

- 20 Freezer Meatballs (see recipe, page 91)
- 1 10¾-ounce can condensed cream of celery soup or 1 10¾-ounce can condensed cream of mushroom soup
- 1 10-ounce package frozen peas with pearl onions
- 1 4-ounce can sliced mushrooms
- 1 teaspoon worcestershire sauce
- ½ teaspoon dried marjoram, crushed
- ¼ cup milk
- ½ cup dairy sour cream
  Hot cooked noodles

In large saucepan combine frozen meatballs, soup, peas, *undrained* mushrooms, worcestershire, and marjoram. Stir in milk. Cover; simmer 20 minutes or till hot. Blend about 1 cup hot mixture into sour cream. Return to hot mixture. Heat through (*do not boil*). Serve over noodles. Serves 4.

Microwave Method: In 2-quart non-metal casserole combine frozen meatballs, soup, peas and onions, mushrooms, worcestershire, and marjoram (omit the milk). Cook, covered, in countertop microwave oven on high power for 12 minutes, stirring twice. Blend 1 cup hot mixture into sour cream. Return to hot mixture. Micro-cook, covered, 1 minute more. Serve as above.

Quick and Easy Stew

25 MINUTES

- 1 24-ounce can beef stew
- 1 11-ounce can condensed cheddar cheese soup
- 1 8¾-ounce can cream-style corn
- ¼ cup water
- 1 package (6) refrigerated biscuits

Preheat oven to 425°. Meanwhile, in saucepan combine beef stew, soup, corn, and water. Cook and stir till boiling. Quickly transfer to 2-quart casserole; immediately place biscuits atop *hot* stew. Bake in 425° oven for 12 minutes or till biscuits are golden. Serves 4.

Jiffy Jambalaya

25 MINUTES

To cut up tomatoes in a hurry, snip them with kitchen shears right in the can –

- ½ cup chopped onion
- ½ cup chopped green pepper
- 2 tablespoons cooking oil
- 1 28-ounce can tomatoes, cut up
- 1 12-ounce can luncheon meat, cubed
- ½ cup water
- 1 teaspoon paprika
- ½ teaspoon dried thyme, crushed
- ½ teaspoon dried oregano, crushed
- ¼ teaspoon salt
- ¼ teaspoon garlic powder
- 3 drops bottled hot pepper sauce
  Dash pepper
- 1½ cups quick-cooking rice

In 3-quart saucepan cook onion and green pepper in hot oil till tender. Stir in remaining ingredients except rice. Bring to boiling. Stir in rice. Cover; simmer 5 minutes more. Stir before serving. Makes 6 servings.

Luncheon Meat Skillet

30 MINUTES

This recipe is a good way to use leftover ham, too –

- 2 16-ounce cans pork and beans in tomato sauce
- 1 20-ounce can sliced apples, drained
- ¼ cup light molasses
- 1 tablespoon minced dried onion
- 1 tablespoon prepared mustard
- 1 tablespoon worcestershire sauce
  Dash ground cloves
- 1 12-ounce can luncheon meat, cubed

In large skillet combine pork and beans, apples, molasses, onion, mustard, worcestershire sauce, and cloves. Stir in luncheon meat. Bring mixture to boiling. Reduce heat and simmer, uncovered, for 15 minutes, stirring frequently to prevent sticking. Serves 4 to 6.

Individual Beef Pies

40 MINUTES

To make cracker crumbs, place crackers in a plastic bag and crush with a rolling pin –

- 1 10-ounce package frozen cut broccoli
- 1 15-ounce can roast beef hash
- ¼ teaspoon ground sage
  Dash pepper
- 1 1¼-ounce envelope cheese sauce mix
- ½ cup crushed rich round crackers (12 crackers)
- 1 tablespoon sesame seed
- ½ teaspoon paprika
- 2 tablespoons butter or margarine, melted

Preheat oven to 400°. Meanwhile, cook broccoli according to package directions; drain. Mix hash, sage, and pepper; press onto bottom and sides of four 1-cup nonmetal casseroles to form a shell. Prepare cheese sauce according to package directions; stir in broccoli. Spoon mixture into hash cups. Mix crackers, sesame seed, and paprika; stir in butter or margarine. Sprinkle atop meat cups. Bake in 400° oven for 12 to 15 minutes. Serves 4.
Microwave Method: Prepare as above *except* cook casseroles, covered, in countertop microwave oven on high power for 6 to 7 minutes or till hot.

Mexican Hash

30 MINUTES

- 2 15-ounce cans roast beef hash
- 1 8-ounce can tomatoes, cut up
- 2 tablespoons rinsed, seeded, and chopped green chili peppers
- 1 cup shredded monterey jack cheese (4 ounces)

In 10-inch skillet stir together hash, *undrained* tomatoes, and chili peppers. Bring to boiling. Reduce heat; simmer, uncovered, stirring often, about 15 minutes or till the excess liquid evaporates. Sprinkle cheese atop hash mixture. Cover and heat about 2 minutes or till cheese melts. Makes 4 servings.

Tamale-Chili Bake

25 MINUTES

- 1   15½-ounce can chili with beans
- 1   12-ounce can whole kernel corn
- ½   cup shredded cheddar cheese (2 ounces)
- ¼   cup catsup
- 1   tablespoon minced dried onion
- 1   15-ounce can tamales in tomato sauce
- 1½   cups Whole Wheat-Honey Biscuit Mix (see recipe, page 92)
- ½   cup milk

Preheat oven to 450°. In saucepan combine chili, *undrained* corn, cheese, catsup, and onion. Bring to boiling. Meanwhile, unwrap tamales, reserving sauce; slice ¼ inch thick. Stir tamale slices and sauce into chili mixture; heat through. Meanwhile, combine Biscuit Mix and milk. Spoon *hot* chili mixture into a 2-quart casserole. Immediately drop mounds of biscuit mixture atop. Bake in 450° oven 10 to 12 minutes. Serves 6.

Mock Lasagna

45 MINUTES

- 2   15-ounce cans beef ravioli in tomato sauce
- 1   beaten egg
- 1   cup cream-style cottage cheese
- ¼   cup grated parmesan cheese
- 1   tablespoon dried parsley flakes
- ⅛   teaspoon garlic powder
- 1   6-ounce package mozzarella cheese slices

Preheat oven to 375°. In a 10x6x2-inch nonmetal baking dish spread *1 can* of the ravioli. Mix egg, cottage cheese, parmesan, parsley, and garlic powder. Spoon over ravioli. Top with *half* the cheese slices. Spoon remaining ravioli over; top with remaining cheese. Bake in 375° oven 30 minutes. Serves 6.
Microwave Method: Assemble as above *except* omit the last layer of cheese. Cook, covered, in countertop microwave oven on high power 10 minutes, turning once. Uncover; add remaining cheese. Micro-cook 1 minute.

Turkey Burgers

30 MINUTES

- 1   tablespoon minced dried onion
- 1   teaspoon instant chicken bouillon granules
- 1   slightly beaten egg
- ½   cup herb-seasoned stuffing mix
- 1   pound ground raw turkey
- 1   cup herb-seasoned stuffing mix, crushed
- 2   to 3 tablespoons cooking oil Cranberry-orange relish

In bowl mix onion, bouillon granules, ¼ cup *water*, and ¼ teaspoon *salt*; stir in egg and the ½ cup stuffing mix. Let stand 5 minutes. Add turkey; mix well. Shape into 5 patties. Coat with the 1 cup crushed stuffing mix. Cook in hot oil 4 to 5 minutes per side. Top with a little cranberry-orange relish. Serves 5.

Corned Beef Skillet

30 MINUTES
Chill the corned beef for easier cutting –

- 1   10¾-ounce can condensed cream of celery soup
- 1   10¾-ounce can condensed cream of chicken soup
- 1½   cups milk
- 1   tablespoon minced dried onion
- 2   teaspoons prepared mustard
- 1   12-ounce can corned beef, cut up
- 1   beaten egg
- 1   cup Corn Bread Mix (see recipe, page 91) or ½ of a 10-ounce package corn bread mix
- 3   tablespoons milk
- 2   tablespoons dried parsley flakes

In 10-inch skillet combine soups, the 1½ cups milk, onion, and mustard. Stir in corned beef. Bring to boiling. Meanwhile, mix egg, Corn Bread Mix, the 3 tablespoons milk, and parsley. Drop batter in 8 mounds atop *boiling* mixture. Reduce heat; cover. Simmer 15 to 20 minutes or till dumplings are cooked. Makes 4 servings.

Majesty Chicken

45 MINUTES

Purchase boned chicken breasts from your butcher to save time –

- 2 medium chicken breasts, skinned and boned
- 2 tablespoons cornstarch
- 2 tablespoons cold water
- 2 teaspoons sugar
- 3 tablespoons cooking oil
- 4 green onions, cut into 1-inch pieces
- 1 16-ounce can bean sprouts or 1 8-ounce can bamboo shoots, drained
- 1½ cups water
- 1 cup sliced celery
- 1 cup sliced fresh mushrooms
- ½ cup Oriental Seasoning (see recipe, page 89)
  Hot cooked rice

Cut chicken breasts into ½-inch-wide strips. Stir together cornstarch, the 2 tablespoons water, and sugar; set aside.

Heat cooking oil in a wok or a large skillet over high heat. Stir-fry chicken and onion about 4 minutes or till meat loses its pink color. Add drained bean sprouts or bamboo shoots, the 1½ cups water, celery, mushrooms, and Oriental Seasoning. Cook and stir over medium heat 5 to 7 minutes or till vegetables are tender. Stir cornstarch mixture. Stir into chicken mixture. Cook and stir about 2 minutes or till mixture is thickened and bubbly. Serve over hot cooked rice. Makes 4 servings.

***Don't forget to use your microwave oven in combination with your conventional range and oven to speed up recipe preparation.** Even if recipe directions call for conventional baking or cooking, use your microwave oven to speed up preliminary chores such as melting butter or chocolate, softening cream cheese, thawing frozen foods, or cooking bacon.*

Raspberry Chicken

40 MINUTES

To broil 5 to 6 inches from the flame in a gas broiler, place chicken directly in broiler pan without the rack –

- 1 2½- to 3-pound broiler-fryer chicken, cut up
  Cooking oil
- 1 10-ounce package frozen red raspberries (quick-thaw pouch)
- 2 teaspoons cornstarch
- ¼ teaspoon ground cinnamon
- 2 tablespoons butter
- 1 teaspoon lemon juice
- ¼ cup sliced almonds

Preheat broiler. Brush chicken with oil. Season with some salt and pepper. Place chicken, skin side down, on broiler rack. Broil 5 to 6 inches from heat 20 minutes or till browned; turn. Broil 10 minutes more. Meanwhile, thaw raspberries; drain, reserving syrup. In saucepan blend syrup into cornstarch; stir in cinnamon. Cook and stir till bubbly. Stir in butter and lemon juice. Gently stir in berries and nuts. Serve with chicken. Makes 4 servings.

Chicken Puffs

35 MINUTES

- 1 10-ounce package (6) frozen patty shells
- ½ cup Chicken Gravy Base (see recipe, page 90)
- 1¾ cups chopped cooked chicken
- 1 8¼-ounce can crushed pineapple, drained
- ½ cup chopped celery
- 1 to 1½ teaspoons curry powder
- ½ cup dairy sour cream

Bake patty shells according to package directions. Meanwhile, in saucepan bring ¾ cup water to boiling; stir in Chicken Gravy Base. Cook and stir till bubbly. Stir in chicken, pineapple, celery, and curry. Fold in sour cream. Heat through (do not boil). Remove tops from shells. Spoon chicken mixture into shells. Replace tops. Makes 6 servings.

Chicken Paprikash

45 MINUTES

3 chicken breasts, split
2 tablespoons cooking oil
2 medium onions, sliced
1 tablespoon paprika
¼ cup dry white wine
½ teaspoon instant chicken
    bouillon granules
½ cup dairy sour cream
1 tablespoon all-purpose flour
    Hot cooked noodles

In 12-inch skillet brown chicken breasts in hot oil about 10 minutes. Drain off fat. Season chicken with some salt and pepper. Add onion to skillet. Blend in paprika. Stir in wine, bouillon granules, and ¼ cup *water*. Bring to boiling. Reduce heat; cover. Simmer 20 minutes. Remove chicken to serving platter; keep warm. Combine sour cream and flour; stir into liquid in skillet. Heat and stir till thickened *(do not boil)*. Serve with chicken over noodles. Serves 6.

Saucy Chicken Livers

30 MINUTES

3 slices bacon
1 pound chicken livers, cut up
1 10½-ounce can condensed cream
    of chicken soup
1 3-ounce package cream cheese,
    cubed
½ cup milk
6 English muffins, split
    Butter or margarine
    Snipped parsley

Preheat broiler. In a 10-inch skillet cook bacon till crisp. Drain, reserving drippings in skillet. Crumble bacon; set aside. Cook chicken livers in drippings 5 minutes or till slightly pink in center. Remove from skillet. In same skillet heat soup till bubbly. Stir in cream cheese, milk, and dash *pepper*. Cook and stir till bubbly. Add livers and bacon; heat 2 to 3 minutes more. Meanwhile, toast muffin halves under broiler; butter. Spoon liver mixture over muffin halves. Top with parsley. Serves 6.

Chicken-Rice Skillet

40 MINUTES
A great way to use leftover chicken –

½ cup chopped celery
2 tablespoons butter or margarine
2½ cups water
1 6-ounce package long grain and
    wild rice mix
2 cups cubed cooked chicken
1 14-ounce can artichoke hearts,
    drained and quartered
1 4-ounce can sliced mushrooms,
    drained

In 10-inch skillet cook celery in butter till tender. Stir in water and rice mix. Bring to boiling; cover. Simmer 15 minutes. Stir in chicken, artichoke hearts, and mushrooms. Cover; simmer 10 minutes more. Serves 4.

Fish Florentine

35 MINUTES

6 frozen breaded fish portions
1 10-ounce package frozen
    chopped spinach
1 11-ounce can condensed cheddar
    cheese soup
1 8-ounce can water chestnuts,
    drained and coarsely chopped
3 tablespoons bacon bits
3 lemon slices, halved (optional)

Prepare fish according to package directions. Meanwhile, cook spinach according to package directions; drain well. In saucepan stir soup, water chestnuts, and bacon bits into spinach; heat through. Turn into 10x6x2-inch baking dish or 1½-quart casserole. Top with fish. Bake in 350° oven for 10 minutes or till hot. Serve with lemon slices, if desired. Makes 6 servings.

Frozen breaded fish is a great base for building quick main dishes. Use breaded fish portions in Fish Florentine, back, and fish sticks for Curried Fishwiches, front (see recipe, page 35).

Sweet-and-Sour Fish

30 MINUTES

- 1 14-ounce package frozen fish sticks
- ¾ cup finely chopped green pepper (1 medium)
- ½ cup finely chopped carrot
- 1 clove garlic, minced
- 2 tablespoons cooking oil
- ¾ cup sugar
- ½ cup red wine vinegar
- 1 tablespoon soy sauce
- 1½ teaspoons instant chicken bouillon granules
- 3 tablespoons cornstarch
   Hot cooked rice

Bake fish sticks according to package directions; cut into 1-inch pieces. Meanwhile, in 3-quart saucepan cook green pepper, carrot, and garlic in oil till tender. Add sugar, vinegar, soy, bouillon granules, and 1¾ cups *water*. Bring to boiling; boil rapidly 1 minute. Mix cornstarch and ¼ cup *cold water*; stir into hot mixture. Cook and stir till bubbly. Stir in fish. Serve over rice. Serves 4 to 6.

Lemon-Sauced Fish

25 MINUTES

- 4 fresh or frozen halibut or salmon steaks
- ¼ cup butter, melted
- ¼ cup sliced green onion
- ¼ teaspoon dried rosemary, crushed
- 2 tablespoons butter
- 2 teaspoons cornstarch
- 1 teaspoon instant chicken bouillon granules
- 1 tablespoon lemon juice

Preheat broiler. Sprinkle fresh or frozen fish with salt and pepper. Broil 4 inches from heat 9 minutes, brushing often with the melted butter. Turn; broil 9 minutes more, brushing with melted butter. Meanwhile, cook onion and rosemary in the 2 tablespoons butter till tender. Stir in cornstarch. Add bouillon granules and ½ cup *water*. Cook and stir till bubbly. Stir in lemon juice. Serve with fish. Serves 4.

Fish Creole

40 MINUTES

- 1 pound fresh or frozen fish fillets
- ½ cup chopped onion
- ½ cup chopped green pepper
- 1 clove garlic, minced
- ¼ cup butter or margarine
- 1 16-ounce can tomatoes, cut up
- 1 tablespoon dried parsley flakes
- 1 tablespoon instant chicken bouillon granules
- ¼ teaspoon bottled hot pepper sauce
- 1 tablespoon cornstarch
- 1 tablespoon cold water
   Hot cooked rice

To thaw frozen fish, place wrapped fish under warm running water for about 10 minutes. Meanwhile, in 10-inch skillet cook onion, green pepper, and garlic in butter or margarine till tender but not brown. Add *undrained* tomatoes, parsley flakes, bouillon granules, and hot pepper sauce. Simmer, covered, for 10 minutes. Blend together cornstarch and water. Stir into tomato mixture. Cook and stir till thickened and bubbly. Cut fish into 1-inch pieces. Add fish to tomato mixture, stirring to coat. Return to boiling; reduce heat. Simmer, covered, for 5 to 7 minutes or till fish flakes easily with a fork. Serve fish mixture over rice. Makes 4 servings.

Microwave Method: To thaw frozen fish, place unwrapped fish in nonmetal dish or pie plate. Cook in countertop microwave oven on high power for 2 minutes or till nearly thawed, turning fish over once. In 2-quart nonmetal casserole combine onion, green pepper, garlic, and butter or margarine. Micro-cook, covered, for 2 minutes. Add *undrained* tomatoes, parsley flakes, bouillon granules, and pepper sauce. Micro-cook, covered, 5 minutes. Blend together cornstarch and water; stir into tomato mixture. Micro-cook, covered, 2 minutes more or till thick, stirring once. Cut fish into 1-inch pieces. Add fish, stirring to coat. Micro-cook, covered, 3 to 4 minutes or till fish flakes easily with fork, stirring once. Serve fish mixture over rice.

Fish with Wine Sauce

30 MINUTES

- 6 fresh or frozen fish steaks (2 pounds total)
- 2 tablespoons butter, melted
- ¼ cup finely chopped onion
- 1 tablespoon butter
- ¼ cup Chicken Gravy Base (see recipe, page 90)
- ¼ cup dairy sour cream
- 1 tablespoon dry sherry
- 1 2½-ounce jar sliced mushrooms, drained

Preheat broiler. Arrange fish on greased cold broiler rack in pan. Brush with *half* the melted butter; sprinkle with ½ teaspoon *salt* and dash *pepper*. Broil 4 inches from heat 9 minutes. Turn. Brush with remaining melted butter. Broil 9 minutes longer. Meanwhile, in small saucepan cook onion in the 1 tablespoon butter 5 minutes. Add Chicken Gravy Base and ½ cup *water*. Cook and stir till bubbly. Mix sour cream and sherry; add to sauce mixture with drained mushrooms. Heat through *(do not boil)*. Serve with fish. Serves 6.

Oriental Shrimp Pie

25 MINUTES

- 6 green onions, cut into ½-inch pieces
- 1 tablespoon butter
- 1 bi-pack chicken chow mein (42 ounces total)
- 2 4½-ounce cans shrimp, drained and deveined
- 1 cup frozen peas
- 2 tablespoons Oriental Seasoning (see recipe, page 89) *or* soy sauce
- 1 package (6) refrigerated biscuits

Preheat oven to 425°. In saucepan cook onion in butter till crisp-tender. Drain vegetables from bi-pack. Add to onion along with can of chow mein gravy, shrimp, peas, and Oriental Seasoning. Heat to boiling. Halve biscuits. Pour *hot* mixture into 1½-quart casserole. Top with biscuits. Bake in 425° oven 10 to 12 minutes. Serves 6.

Seafood Thermidor

15 MINUTES

- ⅓ cup chopped green pepper
- ¼ cup chopped onion
- 2 tablespoons butter or margarine
- 1 10¾-ounce can condensed cream of potato soup
- ½ cup milk
- ½ cup shredded American cheese
- 1 9¼-ounce can tuna or 1 7½-ounce can crab meat, drained, flaked, and cartilage removed or 2 4½-ounce cans shrimp, drained and deveined
- 1 tablespoon dry sherry or lemon juice
  Hot cooked rice

Cook pepper and onion in butter or margarine till tender. Add soup and milk. Cook and stir till hot. Add cheese; stir till melted. Stir in seafood and sherry or lemon juice. Heat through. Serve over rice. Serves 4.

Tuna-Mac Skillet

30 MINUTES

Try using canned salmon, too—

- 1 7¼-ounce package macaroni and cheese dinner mix
- ¾ cup milk
- 2 tablespoons butter or margarine
- 1 3-ounce can sliced mushrooms, drained
- 2 teaspoons dried parsley flakes
- ½ teaspoon paprika
- ½ teaspoon prepared mustard
- 2 6½- or 7-ounce cans tuna, drained and broken into chunks
- 1 cup dairy sour cream

Cook macaroni from mix according to package directions; drain. Meanwhile, in 10-inch skillet combine cheese from mix, milk, and butter or margarine. Stir in drained mushrooms, parsley, paprika, and mustard. Bring to boiling; reduce heat. Simmer 5 minutes, stirring often. Stir in tuna, sour cream, and macaroni. Heat through *(do not boil)*. Serves 4.

MAIN DISHES

Fettucini Carbonara

35 MINUTES

- ½ pound bacon
- ¼ cup whipping cream
- 4 beaten eggs
- 1 pound fettucini, cooked
- ¼ cup butter, melted
- 1 cup grated parmesan cheese
- ¼ cup snipped parsley

Heat oven-proof serving dish in 250° oven. In skillet cook bacon till crisp. Drain; crumble. Heat cream till just warm. Remove from heat; beat in eggs. Toss pasta with butter. Pour egg mixture atop. Toss till well-coated. Add bacon, cheese, and parsley; toss to mix. Sprinkle with pepper. Serves 6.

Tomato Stroganoff

40 MINUTES

In saucepan combine one 15-ounce can *tomato sauce;* one 8-ounce can *tomatoes,* cut up; and one 1-ounce envelope *all-purpose marinade.* Stir in 1½ pounds *beef round steak,* cut into bite-size strips. Let stand 10 minutes. Stir in 2 teaspoons *Italian Seasoning Mix* (see recipe, page 90) and 1 teaspoon *sugar.* Bring to boiling. Reduce heat; simmer, covered, 15 minutes, stirring often. Mix ½ cup *dairy sour cream* and 1 table-spoon *all-purpose flour.* Stir into tomato mixture. Heat through. Serve over hot cooked *fettucini.* Serves 6.

Seafood Newburg

30 MINUTES

For a very special occasion, try lobster –

- 1 10¾-ounce can condensed cream of onion soup
- 1 10¾-ounce can condensed cream of shrimp soup
- 1 cup light cream or milk
- 1 7½-ounce can crab meat, drained, flaked, and cartilage removed or 1 9¼-ounce can tuna, drained and flaked or 2 4½-ounce cans shrimp, drained and deveined
- 1 14½-ounce can cut asparagus or 1 16-ounce can cut green beans or 1 16-ounce can mixed vegetables, drained
- 1 4-ounce can sliced mushrooms, drained
- 1 cup shredded American or process Swiss cheese
- 3 tablespoons dry sherry
- ½ pound fettucini, cooked

In saucepan combine soups and the cream or milk. Heat through. Stir in desired seafood, choice of vegetable, and mushrooms; heat through. Stir in *half* of the cheese and all of the sherry. Cook and stir till cheese is melted. Serve with hot fettucini. Top each serving with remaining cheese. Makes 4 to 6 servings.

Fettucini Carbonara

Corn-Salmon Chowder

25 MINUTES

This creamy chowder, packed full of chunky salmon, is so easy to fix—

- 2 tablespoons chopped onion
- 2 tablespoons butter or margarine
- 1 16-ounce can tomatoes, cut up
- 1 12-ounce can whole kernel corn
- 1 11-ounce can condensed cheddar cheese soup
- 1 cup milk
- 1 16-ounce can salmon, drained, flaked, and skin and bones removed
- 1 tablespoon snipped parsley

In large saucepan cook onion in butter or margarine till tender but not brown. Add *undrained* tomatoes, *undrained* corn, soup, and milk; heat through. Add salmon and parsley; heat through. Makes 5 or 6 servings.

Tuna Chowder

40 MINUTES

Tuna and bacon add a refreshing twist to clam chowder—

- 2 slices bacon, chopped
- ½ cup finely chopped onion
- 1 10¾-ounce can condensed cream of celery soup
- 1 10¾-ounce can condensed Manhattan-style clam chowder
- 1⅓ cups milk (1 soup can)
- ⅔ cup water (½ soup can)
- 1 6½- or 7-ounce can tuna, drained

Cook bacon till lightly brown; add onion and cook till tender. Drain. Stir in soups; blend in milk and water. Break tuna into chunks; add to chowder. Bring to boil; reduce heat and simmer 5 minutes. Garnish with chopped celery leaves or snipped parsley, if desired. Makes 5 or 6 servings.

Turkey-Vegetable Soup

30 MINUTES

The canned ravioli serve as dumplings in this tasty soup fix-up—

- 2 10¾-ounce cans condensed turkey-vegetable soup
- 3 cups water
- 1 cup diced cooked turkey
- 2 teaspoons Italian or Mexican Seasoning Mix (see recipes, page 90)
- 1 15-ounce can cheese ravioli in sauce

In a saucepan combine soup, water, turkey, and Italian or Mexican Seasoning. Bring to boiling; simmer, covered, 15 minutes. Stir in ravioli and sauce; heat through. Makes 6 servings.

Meatball Minestrone

40 MINUTES

- 4 cups water
- 20 Freezer Meatballs (see recipe, page 91)
- 1 15-ounce can great northern beans
- 1 tablespoon instant beef bouillon granules
- 1 tablespoon minced dried onion
- 1 teaspoon dried basil, crushed
- 1 large bay leaf
- ½ of a 7-ounce package spaghetti, broken into 2-inch pieces
- 1 16-ounce can mixed vegetables, drained
- 1 16-ounce can tomatoes, cut up
  Grated parmesan cheese

In a 4-quart Dutch oven combine water, frozen meatballs, *undrained* beans, bouillon granules, onion, basil, and bay leaf. Bring to boiling. Add spaghetti. Simmer, covered, 20 minutes or till meatballs are heated through. Stir in drained mixed vegetables and *undrained* tomatoes. Heat through. Serve with parmesan. Makes 8 servings.

Prepare easy Meatball Minestrone for a from-scratch flavor in only 40 minutes.

SOUPS

Chicken-Cheese Soup

30 MINUTES

If you don't have any green onion on hand, substitute chopped white onion—

- 1 cup coarsely shredded carrot (2 medium)
- ¼ cup sliced green onion
- 3 tablespoons butter or margarine
- ¼ cup all-purpose flour
- 2 cups milk
- 1 10½-ounce can condensed chicken broth
- ½ teaspoon worcestershire sauce
- ⅛ teaspoon pepper
- 1½ cups cubed cooked chicken
- 1 cup shredded cheddar cheese (4 ounces)

In medium saucepan cook carrot and green onion in butter or margarine about 10 minutes or till tender but not brown. Blend in flour. Add milk, chicken broth, worcestershire sauce, and pepper. Cook and stir till thickened and bubbly. Stir in chicken and cheese; cook and stir over low heat till cheese melts. Makes 4 servings.

Chicken-Tomato Soup

20 MINUTES

Serve this hearty chicken and vegetable combo when you need a hot soup on the double—

- 1 16-ounce can tomatoes, cut up
- 1 10½-ounce can condensed chicken with rice soup
- 1 8½-ounce can peas
- ½ cup water
- 2 teaspoons minced dried onion
- 1 teaspoon dried green pepper flakes
- ¼ teaspoon sugar
- 2 5-ounce cans boned chicken, drained and cut up

In large saucepan combine *undrained* tomatoes, soup, *undrained* peas, water, onion, green pepper flakes, sugar, and dash *pepper*. Bring mixture to boiling. Reduce heat; cover. Simmer 10 minutes. Carefully stir in chicken. Cook till heated through. Makes 4 servings.

Lima-Corned Beef Soup

20 MINUTES

The tender cubes of corned beef really liven up this time-saving soup—

- 2½ cups milk
- 1 11½-ounce can condensed bean with bacon soup
- 1 12-ounce can corned beef, cubed
- 1 8½-ounce can lima beans
- 1 8¼-ounce can sliced carrots

In a large saucepan blend milk into soup. Stir in corned beef, *undrained* beans, and *undrained* carrots. Simmer, uncovered, about 10 minutes. Makes 4 to 6 servings.

Polish Sausage Soup

45 MINUTES

Large, flat soup bowls are perfect for serving this spicy sausage soup—

- 1 cup chopped celery
- 2 tablespoons butter or margarine
- 2 13¾-ounce cans beef broth
- 1 tablespoon minced dried onion
- ½ teaspoon dry mustard
- ¼ teaspoon garlic powder
- ¼ teaspoon dried oregano, crushed
- ¼ teaspoon dried basil, crushed
- 1 pound Polish sausage, sliced
- 1 16-ounce can cut green beans, drained
- 1 tablespoon cornstarch
- 1 tablespoon cold water
- ½ cup shredded mozzarella cheese (2 ounces)

In large saucepan cook celery in butter or margarine till tender. Add beef broth, onion, dry mustard, garlic powder, oregano, and basil. Heat to boiling; stir in Polish sausage and green beans. Reduce heat; simmer, covered, 15 minutes, stirring occasionally. Combine cornstarch and water; stir into mixture. Cook and stir till slightly thickened and bubbly. Sprinkle cheese over individual servings. Makes 4 servings.

Macaroni-Cheese Soup

35 MINUTES

Here's a main-dish soup that conveniently uses a macaroni and cheese dinner mix—

- 1 10-ounce package frozen mixed vegetables
- 1 7¼-ounce package macaroni and cheese dinner mix
- ¼ cup butter or margarine
- 3 tablespoons all-purpose flour
- 2 13¾-ounce cans chicken broth
- 1 cup beer
- 1½ cups diced fully cooked ham (8 ounces)

Thaw vegetables in strainer under hot running water. In large saucepan cook the macaroni from the dinner mix in boiling salted water till tender; drain and set aside. Meanwhile, in another saucepan melt the butter or margarine. Blend in the flour and the cheese sauce packet from the dinner mix. Gradually stir in the chicken broth and beer. Add thawed vegetables and ham. Cook and stir till thickened and bubbly. Stir in the cooked macaroni. Makes 6 servings.

Beans-and-Franks Soup

40 MINUTES

Canned pork and beans become something special when you add frankfurters and chili sauce—

- ¾ cup chopped celery
- ¾ cup chopped onion
- ½ cup water
- ½ teaspoon salt
-    Dash pepper
- 2 16-ounce cans pork and beans in tomato sauce
- 2 cups milk
- ¼ cup chili sauce
- 12 ounces frankfurters, sliced

In a saucepan combine celery, onion, water, salt, and pepper. Cook 10 minutes or till vegetables are tender. Add beans and mash slightly. Stir in milk, then chili sauce. Add frankfurters; heat through. Makes 6 servings.

Sausage-Garbanzo Soup

45 MINUTES

Vary the spiciness of this soup by using hot or mild sausage—

- 1 pound bulk Italian sausage
- ½ cup chopped onion
- 3½ cups water
- 1 15-ounce can garbanzo beans
- 1½ cups cubed potatoes
- 4 teaspoons instant beef bouillon granules
- 1 teaspoon paprika

In large saucepan or Dutch oven cook sausage and onion till meat is browned and onion is tender; drain. Stir in water, *undrained* beans, potatoes, bouillon granules, and paprika. Bring to boiling; reduce heat. Simmer, covered, 30 minutes or till potatoes are tender; stir occasionally. Makes 6 to 8 servings.

Beef-Vegetable Soup

25 MINUTES

When minutes matter, this hearty goulash-like soup can't be beat—

- 1 pound ground beef
- ½ cup chopped onion
- ½ cup Beef Gravy Base (see recipe, page 90)
- ½ teaspoon salt
- 3 cups water
- 2 teaspoons worcestershire sauce
- 1 10-ounce package frozen peas and carrots
- 1 cup fine noodles
- 1 8-ounce can tomatoes, cut up

In a large saucepan cook beef and onion till beef is browned and onion is tender. Drain. Stir in Gravy Base and salt. Stir in water and worcestershire sauce; bring to boiling. Add frozen peas and carrots, noodles, and *undrained* tomatoes. Return to boiling. Simmer, covered, 10 minutes or till noodles and vegetables are tender. Serves 4.

Burgers Divan

35 MINUTES

- 4 hamburger buns, split
- 3 slices bacon
- ¼ cup chopped onion
- 1 teaspoon worcestershire sauce
- ½ teaspoon dry mustard
- ¼ teaspoon dried oregano, crushed
- 1 pound ground beef
- ¼ cup mayonnaise
- 2 teaspoons milk
- 1 small zucchini, thinly sliced
- 4 thick slices tomato
- 2 tablespoons grated parmesan cheese

Preheat broiler. Toast buns in broiler; set aside. Meanwhile, in skillet cook bacon till crisp; drain, reserving drippings. Crumble bacon. Cook onion in drippings till tender. Mix bacon, onion, worcestershire, mustard, oregano, and ¾ teaspoon *salt*; add beef. Mix well. Shape into four ½-inch-thick patties. Broil 3 to 4 inches from heat 4 minutes; turn. Broil 3 to 4 minutes more. Combine mayonnaise and milk. Top each burger with a few slices of zucchini and 1 tomato slice. Dollop mayonnaise mixture atop. Sprinkle with cheese. Broil 1 minute. Serve on buns. Serves 4.

Sprout Burgers

25 MINUTES

- 4 hamburger buns, split
- 2 slightly beaten eggs
- ¾ cup soft bread crumbs
- 2 tablespoons chopped onion
- 2 tablespoons soy sauce
- 1 tablespoon sugar
- 1 clove garlic, minced
- ⅛ teaspoon ground ginger
- 1 pound ground beef
- 1 cup snipped fresh or canned bean sprouts

Preheat broiler. Toast buns in broiler; set aside. Combine next 7 ingredients. Add ground beef and bean sprouts; mix well. Shape into 4 patties. Broil 4 inches from heat for 4 minutes. Turn; broil 4 to 5 minutes more. Serve on toasted buns. Makes 4 servings.

Greek Pocket Steaks

35 MINUTES

These are extra easy to eat because the filling is stuffed inside pita bread –

- 1 tablespoon olive or cooking oil
- 1 tablespoon red wine vinegar
- ½ teaspoon dried oregano, crushed
- ¼ teaspoon salt
- 1 small cucumber, seeded and chopped
- 1 medium tomato, chopped
- 2 pita bread rounds
- 1 medium onion, sliced
- 1 tablespoon olive or cooking oil
- 4 beef cubed steaks (1 pound total)
- ½ teaspoon salt
  Dash pepper
- 1 cup shredded lettuce
  Pimiento-stuffed olives (optional)

Preheat oven to 250°. In medium mixing bowl combine 1 tablespoon olive or cooking oil, red wine vinegar, oregano, and ¼ teaspoon salt. Stir in chopped cucumber and tomato. Cut pita bread rounds in half crosswise. Place on baking sheet; warm in 250° oven. Meanwhile, in skillet cook onion in 1 tablespoon olive or cooking oil till tender but not brown. Push onion aside. Cook beef steaks 2 minutes. Turn; cook 2 minutes more or till done. Sprinkle with the ½ teaspoon salt and pepper. Place 1 steak and some of the cooked onions in each bread round half. Toss lettuce with cucumber-tomato mixture; spoon atop meat and onions in each bread round half. Serve with olives, if desired. Makes 4 sandwiches.

When you need a truly impressive sandwich, try Burgers Divan, bottom left; Greek Pocket Steaks, top; or Ham-Apple Turnovers, bottom right (see recipe, page 34).

Spicy Meatball Rolls

30 MINUTES

- 20 Freezer Meatballs (see recipe, page 91)
- 1 15½-ounce jar meatless spaghetti sauce
- 1 medium onion, sliced
- 1 medium green pepper, cut into strips
- 1 tablespoon butter or margarine
- 5 individual French rolls or hoagie rolls, split
- ¼ cup grated parmesan cheese

Mix frozen meatballs and spaghetti sauce. Simmer, covered, 20 to 25 minutes. Meanwhile, cook onion and pepper in butter till tender. Place four meatballs on each roll bottom. Spoon some onion mixture over meatballs. Spoon sauce atop; top with cheese. Add roll tops. Makes 5.

Hamburger Stack-Ups

40 MINUTES

- 8 hamburger buns, split
- 1 beaten egg
- ¾ cup soft bread crumbs
- 1 pound ground beef
- ½ cup mayonnaise
- 4 eggs
- 3 tablespoons milk
- 2 tablespoons butter
- 8 slices American cheese
- 8 lettuce leaves
- 1 avocado, peeled, seeded, and cut into 8 slices

Preheat broiler. Toast buns in broiler. Meanwhile, combine the 1 egg, crumbs, and ½ teaspoon *salt*. Add beef; mix. Shape into 8 thin hamburger patties. Spread mayonnaise on cut surfaces of buns; set aside. Broil meat patties 3 to 4 inches from heat for 3 to 4 minutes on each side. Meanwhile, beat together the 4 eggs, milk, and ¼ teaspoon *salt*. In skillet scramble eggs in butter, cooking just till set. Place cheese atop burgers; return to broiler 1 minute to melt cheese. Place lettuce and meat patty on bottom half of each bun; top each with spoonful of egg and an avocado slice. Add bun top. Makes 8.

Ham-Apple Turnovers

35 MINUTES
These sandwiches are pictured on page 33 –

- 1 12-ounce package (6) refrigerated apple turnovers
- 1½ cups diced fully cooked ham
- 3 tablespoons bottled barbecue sauce
- 1 8½-ounce can applesauce (optional)

Preheat oven to 400°. Meanwhile, unroll turnover pastry; separate into sections. Roll each section into a 5½-inch square. Place ¼ cup ham in center of each square. Mix apple filling from turnovers and barbecue sauce; spoon 1 tablespoon mixture over ham on each square. (Save icing from turnovers for another use.) Moisten edges. Fold pastry in half diagonally to form a triangle; press edges to seal. Place on baking sheet. Bake in 400° oven for 10 to 12 minutes. In saucepan heat applesauce, if desired. Spoon over turnovers. Makes 6.

Open-Face Ham Broil

25 MINUTES

- 6 slices white bread
- 6 *thin* veal cutlets (12 ounces total)
- 1 beaten egg
- ⅓ cup fine dry bread crumbs
- 2 tablespoons cooking oil
- 6 slices boiled cooked ham
- ¼ cup creamy Italian salad dressing
- 3 slices cheddar or Swiss cheese, halved crosswise

Preheat broiler. Toast bread on one side under broiler. Meanwhile, season veal with some salt and pepper; dip in egg, then in bread crumbs. In skillet over medium heat brown veal in hot oil 2 minutes per side. Place bread, toasted side down, on broiler pan. Top each with a ham slice; broil 3 to 4 inches from heat for 1 to 2 minutes. Top *each* with some of the dressing, a veal cutlet, and half a cheese slice. Broil 1 to 2 minutes more. Makes 6.

SANDWICHES

Mustard-Ham Rolls

35 MINUTES

1 package (8) refrigerated crescent rolls
8 slices boiled ham
4 ounces liver sausage
½ cup mayonnaise
½ cup sweet pickle relish, drained
2 teaspoons prepared mustard

Preheat oven to 375°. Unroll crescent rolls, separating into triangles. Place a slice of ham on each triangle. Spread each with some liver sausage. Combine mayonnaise, pickle relish, and mustard; spread atop sausage. Roll each triangle, beginning at wide end. Shape into a crescent. Place on baking sheet. Bake in 375° oven 15 minutes. Makes 8.

Barbecue Sandwiches

25 MINUTES

6 hamburger buns or English muffins, split
1 10¾-ounce can condensed tomato soup
2 tablespoons vinegar
1 tablespoon sugar
1 tablespoon worcestershire sauce
2 teaspoons minced dried onion
1½ teaspoons prepared mustard
Several dashes bottled hot pepper sauce
8 ounces thinly sliced cooked pork or beef (1½ cups)

Preheat broiler. Toast buns in broiler. Meanwhile, in saucepan mix soup, vinegar, sugar, worcestershire, onion, mustard, pepper sauce, and 2 tablespoons *water*. Bring to boiling; reduce heat. Simmer, covered, 10 minutes. Stir in meat; heat through. Spoon over buns. Makes 6.
Microwave Method: Toast buns as above. In 2-quart nonmetal casserole combine soup, vinegar, sugar, worcestershire, onion, mustard, and pepper sauce. (Omit water.) Cook, uncovered, in countertop microwave oven on high power for 4 minutes, stirring twice. Stir in meat. Micro-cook 4 minutes. Serve over buns.

Salmon-Slaw Buns

15 MINUTES

1 7¾-ounce can salmon, drained, flaked, and skin and bones removed
1 cup coleslaw
6 onion rolls, split
2 medium tomatoes, sliced
1 cup alfalfa sprouts or shredded lettuce

Combine salmon and slaw; spread ⅓ cup mixture on each of six roll bottoms. Sprinkle tomato slices with salt; place atop salmon mixture. Top with sprouts or lettuce; add roll tops. Makes 6.

Curried Fishwiches

25 MINUTES
These muffin stacks are shown on page 23 –

2 eggs
6 English muffins, split
Butter or margarine
2 8-ounce packages frozen breaded fish sticks
3 tablespoons butter
3 tablespoons all-purpose flour
¾ teaspoon curry powder
¾ teaspoon dry mustard
2¼ cups milk
1 teaspoon minced dried onion
1 cup cubed or shredded American cheese (4 ounces)
1 tablespoon lemon juice

Preheat broiler. In saucepan cover eggs with cold water. Bring to boiling. Reduce heat to just below simmering. Cover; cook 15 minutes. Meanwhile, toast muffins under broiler; remove and spread with butter. Broil fish 4 inches from heat for 4 to 6 minutes. Meanwhile, melt the 3 tablespoons butter. Blend in flour, curry, mustard, ½ teaspoon *salt*, and ⅛ teaspoon *pepper*. Add milk and onion. Cook and stir till mixture thickens. Stir in cheese; heat and stir till melted. Cool eggs under cold running water. Peel and chop eggs; stir into sauce. Drizzle fish with lemon juice. Place fish on muffin bottoms; spoon sauce over. Top with muffin tops or serve open face. Makes 6 servings.

Swiss Bratwurst Melt

30 MINUTES

- 2 tablespoons butter or margarine
- 4 teaspoons all-purpose flour
- ½ teaspoon dry mustard
- ¼ teaspoon salt
- ¾ cup milk
- ¾ cup shredded Swiss cheese (3 ounces)
- 1 8-ounce can sauerkraut, drained
- 4 fully cooked bratwurst, Polish sausage, frankfurters, or smoked sausage links
- 4 slices pumpernickel bread
- 4 slices tomato

Preheat broiler. In small saucepan melt butter or margarine. Stir in flour, mustard, and salt. Add milk; cook and stir till thickened and bubbly. Stir in cheese till melted; fold in sauerkraut. Cover; keep warm over low heat. Halve sausages lengthwise. Broil, cut side down, 3 to 5 inches from heat for 2 to 3 minutes. Meanwhile, toast bread in toaster. To assemble sandwich, place 2 sausage halves on each bread slice. Top each with a tomato slice. Spoon one-fourth of the cheese sauce over each. Garnish with green pepper rings, if desired. Makes 4 sandwiches.

Turkey-Pita Rounds

35 MINUTES

- 2 cups diced cooked turkey
- ½ cup cranberry-orange relish
- ½ cup finely chopped celery
- ½ cup mayonnaise or salad dressing
- ½ teaspoon salt
  Dash pepper
- 4 pita bread rounds, halved crosswise

Preheat oven to 375°. Meanwhile, in mixing bowl combine turkey, cranberry-orange relish, celery, mayonnaise or salad dressing, salt, and pepper. Spoon some filling into each of the pita round halves. Place on baking sheet. Bake in 375° oven about 10 minutes or till hot. Serves 4.

Chicken-Asparagus Muffin Stacks

30 MINUTES
Drape asparagus with the delicate wine sauce for this extra-special sandwich idea –

- 8 rusks or English muffins, split
- 1 10-ounce package frozen asparagus spears
- ⅔ cup Chicken Gravy Base (see recipe, page 90)
- 1½ teaspoons minced dried onion
- ½ teaspoon prepared mustard
  Dash bottled hot pepper sauce
- 1 cup water
- ¼ cup dry white wine
- 1 teaspoon lemon juice
- 1½ cups diced cooked chicken

Preheat broiler. Toast rusks or muffins. Meanwhile, cook asparagus according to package directions. At the same time, in saucepan combine Gravy Base, onion, mustard, and hot pepper sauce. Stir in water. Cook and stir over medium heat till thickened and bubbly. Stir in wine and lemon juice. Stir in chicken; heat through. Drain asparagus. For each sandwich, top rusk round or muffin half with a little chicken mixture. Top with another rusk round or muffin top, a few asparagus spears, and more chicken mixture. Makes 4.

Microwave Method: Toast rusks or muffins as above. With sharp knife, make 2 or 3 slashes in the package of asparagus. Place whole package in countertop microwave oven. Cook on high power for 5 minutes. Keep warm. In 4-cup glass measure combine Gravy Base, onion, mustard, hot pepper sauce, and water. Micro-cook, uncovered, 3 to 4 minutes or till thickened and bubbly, stirring every minute. Stir in wine and lemon juice. Add chicken; micro-cook, uncovered, 2 to 3 minutes more, stirring every minute. Assemble as above.

Turn an ordinary luncheon into a sophisticated meal with Chicken-Asparagus Muffin Stacks, front. And try Zucchini Skillet, back, (see recipe, page 50) the next time you want a spicy vegetable side dish –

Salmon-Potato Salad

30 MINUTES

    ¾ cup dairy sour cream
    ¼ cup chili sauce
    3 tablespoons French salad
       dressing
    2 teaspoons lemon juice
    1 16-ounce can sliced potatoes,
       chilled and drained
    1 cup sliced celery
    ½ cup sliced radishes
    1 tablespoon sliced green onion
    1 16-ounce can salmon, chilled,
       drained, broken up, and skin
       and bones removed
       Lettuce cups

Combine sour cream, chili sauce,
French dressing, lemon juice, and ½
teaspoon *salt*. Stir in potatoes, celery,
radishes, and onion. Add salmon; toss.
Spoon into lettuce cups. Serves 4 to 6.

Crab-Sesame Toss

30 MINUTES

    1 tablespoon sesame seeds
    3 tablespoons mayonnaise or
       salad dressing
    3 tablespoons French salad
       dressing
    2 tablespoons grated parmesan
       cheese
    1 teaspoon sugar
    1 teaspoon vinegar
    4 cups torn lettuce
    1 11-ounce can mandarin orange
       sections, drained
    1 7½-ounce can crab meat,
       drained, broken into chunks,
       and cartilage removed
    ½ medium cucumber, sliced
    ½ cup chopped green pepper
    2 green onions, sliced

In skillet over medium heat toast
sesame seeds for 3 to 5 minutes or till
lightly browned, stirring often; set
aside. Combine mayonnaise, French
dressing, cheese, sugar, vinegar, and
¼ teaspoon *salt*; stir in sesame seed.
Combine lettuce, orange sections,
crab, cucumber, green pepper, and
green onions in salad bowl. Pour dressing mixture atop. Toss. Serves 4.

Scallop Chef's Salad

30 MINUTES

    1 12-ounce package frozen
       scallops
    1 clove garlic, halved
    4 cups torn lettuce
    3 cups torn romaine
    1 cup sliced celery
    4 ounces mozzarella cheese, cut
       into thin strips
   12 cherry tomatoes, halved
       Thousand island salad dressing

Cook scallops in boiling salted water 3
to 5 minutes or till done; drain. Place in
plastic bag and seal; chill in freezer 20
minutes. Meanwhile, rub salad bowl
with cut side of garlic; discard garlic. In
bowl combine lettuce, romaine, celery,
cheese, and tomatoes. Top with scallops. Pour desired amount of dressing
over. Toss. Serves 6.

Shrimp-Avocado Salad

25 MINUTES

    1 small avocado, peeled, pitted,
       and cut up
    ½ cup buttermilk
    1 3-ounce package cream cheese
    1 tablespoon lemon juice
    1 small clove garlic
    ¼ teaspoon bottled hot pepper
       sauce
    6 cups torn lettuce
    1 pound shelled shrimp, cooked
       and drained
   18 cherry tomatoes, halved
    4 ounces Swiss cheese, cut into
       strips

In blender container place first six ingredients and ½ teaspoon *salt*; cover
and blend till smooth. Arrange lettuce
in salad bowl. Arrange shrimp, tomatoes, and cheese atop. Sprinkle with
a little pepper. Toss with avocado mixture to serve. Makes 6 servings.

Try these two colorful salads – Shrimp-
Avocado Salad, *top, and* Fruit Medley
Salad, *bottom (see recipe, page 44).*

Cucumber-Tuna Boats

20 MINUTES

2 medium cucumbers
1 6½- or 7-ounce can tuna, chilled, drained, and flaked
¾ cup shredded American cheese (3 ounces)
½ cup finely chopped celery
⅓ cup mayonnaise
2 tablespoons sweet pickle relish
1 tablespoon finely chopped onion
1 teaspoon lemon juice
Paprika

Cut cucumbers in half lengthwise; scrape out seeds. Cut a thin slice from bottom so cucumbers will not rock; sprinkle cavities with a little salt. Combine tuna, cheese, celery, mayonnaise, pickle relish, onion, and lemon juice. Fill shells with tuna mixture. Sprinkle with paprika. Makes 4 servings.

Salad Con Carne

30 MINUTES

1 pound bulk Italian sausage
2 tablespoons Beef Gravy Base (see recipe, page 90)
1 cup water
6 cups torn lettuce or spinach
1 large tomato, cut into wedges
1 cup shredded cheddar cheese (4 ounces)
½ medium onion, thinly sliced and separated into rings
½ small green pepper, cut into strips
½ cup sliced pitted ripe olives
1 cup corn chips, coarsely crushed or 2 taco shells, coarsely crushed

In 10-inch skillet brown meat; drain off excess fat. Stir in Gravy Base; add water. Bring to boiling, stirring constantly. Reduce heat; simmer 10 minutes, stirring occasionally. Meanwhile, in large salad bowl combine lettuce, tomato, cheese, onion rings, green pepper, and olives; toss. Spoon hot meat sauce over all; top with crushed corn chips or taco shells. Makes 6 servings.

Sausage-Bean Toss

35 MINUTES

¼ cup salad oil
¼ cup wine vinegar
½ teaspoon sugar
½ teaspoon worcestershire sauce
¼ teaspoon dried savory, crushed
Dash garlic powder
1 16-ounce can cut wax beans, drained
1 16-ounce can cut green beans, drained
4 ounces summer sausage, cut into chunks
1 3-ounce can sliced mushrooms, drained
2 ounces cheddar or Swiss cheese, cubed (½ cup)
Lettuce cups

In screw-top jar combine oil, vinegar, sugar, worcestershire, savory, garlic powder, and ¼ teaspoon *salt*. Cover; shake well. Combine beans, sausage, and mushrooms; pour dressing over. Mix well. Cover; chill in freezer 20 minutes; drain. Add cheese; toss. Serve in lettuce cups. Serves 4.

Chili-Corn Salad

20 MINUTES

6 cups torn salad greens
1 15-ounce can pinto beans with chili sauce, chilled
1 12-ounce can whole kernel corn with sweet peppers, chilled and drained
4 ounces sliced hard salami, cut into 2-inch strips
2 ounces monterey jack cheese, cubed (½ cup)
½ cup chopped celery
2 tablespoons sliced green onion
¼ cup mayonnaise or salad dressing
½ teaspoon worcestershire sauce

In large salad bowl combine greens, pinto beans, corn, salami, cheese, celery, and onion; toss lightly. In small bowl combine mayonnaise, worcestershire sauce, and ¼ teaspoon *salt*. Toss mayonnaise mixture with vegetables and meat. Makes 6 servings.

Cervelat-Bean Salad

25 MINUTES

1 16-ounce can garbanzo beans, drained
¼ cup salad oil or olive oil
¼ cup white wine vinegar
½ teaspoon salt
½ teaspoon dry mustard
⅛ teaspoon pepper
6 cups torn spinach
½ pound cervelat or other summer sausage, cut into strips
1 small red onion, thinly sliced and halved

Chill beans in freezer 20 minutes. Meanwhile, prepare dressing in screw-top jar; combine oil, vinegar, salt, mustard, and pepper. Cover and shake well. In large bowl layer spinach, cervelat, chilled beans, and onion. Shake dressing well; drizzle over salad. Toss lightly. If desired, sprinkle chopped chives atop. Makes 4 servings.

Curried Chicken Salad

30 MINUTES

This salad is a great way to use up leftover turkey, too –

1 large orange
1 medium banana
4 cups torn salad greens
2 cups cubed cooked chicken
½ of an 8-ounce can (½ cup) jellied cranberry sauce, chilled and cut into ½-inch cubes
¼ cup light raisins
¼ cup salted peanuts
½ cup mayonnaise or salad dressing
½ cup orange yogurt
½ to 1 teaspoon curry powder

Section orange over bowl to catch juice. Slice banana diagonally and dip in reserved orange juice. Place salad greens in large salad bowl. Arrange orange sections, banana, chicken, the cranberry cubes, raisins, and peanuts atop greens. For dressing, combine mayonnaise, yogurt, and curry. Toss salad to serve; pass dressing with salad. Makes 4 servings.

Chicken-Avocado Salad à l'Orange

35 MINUTES
This salad, pictured on page 43, gets its tangy flavor from the oranges –

3 tablespoons frozen orange juice concentrate
1 tablespoon sugar
1 tablespoon vinegar
⅛ teaspoon dry mustard
    Few drops bottled hot pepper sauce
¼ cup mayonnaise or salad dressing
2 cups cubed cooked chicken
1 cup bias-sliced celery
½ cup sliced pitted ripe olives
2 medium avocados, peeled, pitted, and sliced
2 medium oranges, peeled and sectioned
    Leaf lettuce
¼ cup slivered almonds, toasted (optional)

For dressing, in large mixing bowl stir together orange juice concentrate, sugar, vinegar, dry mustard, pepper sauce, and dash *salt*. Stir in mayonnaise. Add chicken, celery, and olives; toss lightly. To serve, arrange avocado slices and orange sections in individual lettuce-lined bowls. Mound chicken mixture in center. Sprinkle with almonds, if desired. Serves 3 or 4.

Carefully prepare the salad greens for your tossed salad to ensure its success. To prepare lettuce for use, remove and discard wilted outer leaves. For more thorough rinsing, remove the core from head lettuce, or separate leafy lettuce. Rinse the greens in cold water and drain. Place leafy greens in a clean kitchen towel or paper toweling, and pat or toss gently to remove clinging water. Tear – don't cut – greens into bite-size pieces. Tearing exposes the interior and allows dressing to be absorbed by the greens.

Polynesian Ham Toss

30 MINUTES

1   15½-ounce can pineapple
     chunks
4   cups torn lettuce
2   cups cubed fully cooked ham
½   cup sliced water chestnuts
2   tablespoons sliced green onion
⅓   cup peanuts
½   cup dairy sour cream
½   teaspoon ground ginger

Drain pineapple, reserving 2 tablespoons syrup. In salad bowl combine
pineapple chunks, lettuce, ham, water
chestnuts, sliced green onion, and
peanuts. Combine sour cream, ginger,
and reserved pineapple syrup. Pour
over salad; toss. Makes 4 servings.

Spinach-Egg Scramble

35 MINUTES

3   eggs
2   tablespoons milk
1   tablespoon dried parsley flakes
⅛   teaspoon salt
     Dash pepper
1   tablespoon butter or margarine
¼   cup mayonnaise or salad
     dressing
¼   cup dairy sour cream
2   tablespoons milk
1   teaspoon prepared mustard
¼   teaspoon curry powder
4   cups torn spinach
2   cups torn bibb lettuce
4   ounces boiled ham slices, cut
     into strips

Beat together eggs, 2 tablespoons milk,
parsley flakes, salt, and pepper. In 10-
inch skillet over medium-low heat, melt
butter or margarine. Pour in egg mixture; cook over low heat, without stirring, till set. Remove from skillet and cut
eggs into ½-inch strips; chill in freezer 15
minutes. In small bowl combine
mayonnaise or salad dressing, sour
cream, 2 tablespoons milk, mustard,
and curry powder. Chill mixture in
freezer while preparing the salad.
   In salad bowl combine spinach, bibb
lettuce, ham, and egg strips. Serve with
chilled dressing. Serves 4.

Peach-and-Pork Cups

45 MINUTES

⅓   cup peach yogurt
¼   cup mayonnaise or salad
     dressing
½   teaspoon dried thyme, crushed
½   teaspoon dried basil, crushed
¼   teaspoon salt
1   8¾-ounce can peach slices,
     chilled, well-drained, and
     chopped
2   cups diced cooked pork
½   cup chopped celery
2   large green peppers

For dressing, in bowl combine yogurt,
mayonnaise or salad dressing, thyme,
basil, salt, and dash *pepper*. Pat
peaches dry with paper toweling; fold
into dressing along with pork and celery. Chill in freezer 20 minutes. Just before serving, cut green peppers in half
lengthwise; remove seeds and rinse.
Cut a small slice from the bottom of each
half so cups will rest evenly on plate; fill
with pork mixture. Makes 4 servings.

Royal Reuben Salad

20 MINUTES

6   cups torn leaf lettuce
2   3-ounce packages thinly sliced
     corned beef, cut into strips
4   ounces cubed Swiss cheese
     (1 cup)
1   cup seasoned croutons
¾   to 1 cup thousand island salad
     dressing
1   8-ounce can sauerkraut, chilled
     and drained
½   teaspoon caraway seed

Place lettuce in large bowl. Arrange
corned beef, Swiss cheese, and
croutons atop lettuce. Combine dressing, sauerkraut, and caraway seed;
spoon over salad and toss till well
coated. Serves 6.

Spinach-Egg Scramble, *top left;* Royal Reu-
ben Salad, *right; and* Chicken-Avocado
Salad à l'Orange, *bottom left (see recipe,
page 41) are ideal for cool summer meals.*

Fruit Medley Salad

30 MINUTES

This attractive fresh fruit salad is pictured on page 39 –

- 4 ounces prosciutto, thinly sliced and cut up
- ½ honeydew melon, cut into balls
- ½ cantaloupe, cut into balls
- 1 large peach, sliced
- 1 cup strawberries, halved
  Leaf lettuce
- ¼ cup dairy sour cream
- ¼ cup mayonnaise or salad dressing
- ¼ cup crumbled blue cheese
- 2 teaspoons milk

Arrange prosciutto, melon balls, peach slices, and strawberries on lettuce-lined platter. In small mixing bowl combine sour cream, mayonnaise or salad dressing, blue cheese, and milk. Serve with salad. Makes 4 servings.

Pepperoni Salad

40 MINUTES

- 1 7-ounce package thin spaghetti, broken up
- ⅓ cup mayonnaise or salad dressing
- 2 tablespoons prepared mustard
- 1 tablespoon dried parsley flakes
- 3 medium tomatoes, chopped (2 cups)
- 2 3-ounce packages sliced pepperoni, quartered
- 4 ounces cubed cheddar cheese (1 cup)
- ½ cup chopped green pepper
  Lettuce cups

Cook spaghetti in boiling salted water according to package directions; drain. Cover with very cold water; let stand 5 minutes. Drain. In large bowl combine mayonnaise or salad dressing, mustard, and parsley flakes. Add cooked spaghetti, chopped tomatoes, pepperoni, cheddar cheese, and green pepper, tossing lightly to coat. To serve, spoon into lettuce cups. Makes 6 to 8 servings.

Hot Oriental Salad

30 MINUTES

- 3 cups torn lettuce
- 3 cups torn spinach
- 2 medium tomatoes, cut into wedges
- ¾ cup chopped green pepper
- ½ cup sliced radishes
- ⅓ cup sliced green onion
- ¼ cup salad oil
- ¼ cup vinegar
- 1 0.6-ounce envelope Italian salad dressing mix
- 4 teaspoons sugar
- 1 tablespoon soy sauce
- 1 16-ounce can chop suey vegetables, drained

In large salad bowl combine lettuce, spinach, tomatoes, green pepper, radishes, and green onion. In saucepan combine salad oil, vinegar, dry dressing mix, sugar, and soy sauce. Stir in chop suey vegetables. Heat to boiling; pour over salad mixture. Toss gently to coat. Makes 6 to 8 servings.
Microwave Method: Assemble salad as above *except* in 4-cup glass measure combine oil, vinegar, dressing mix, sugar, and soy. Stir in chop suey vegetables. Cook, uncovered, in countertop microwave oven on high power for 1 to 2 minutes or till boiling; pour over salad mixture. Serve as above.

Quick Apple Mold

35 MINUTES

- 1 3-ounce package lemon-flavored gelatin
- 1 cup boiling water
- 2 cups ice cubes
- 1 tablespoon lemon juice
- 1 small apple, chopped
- ⅓ cup chopped celery
- ¼ cup chopped walnuts

Dissolve gelatin in boiling water. Stir in ice cubes and lemon juice. Stir about 3 minutes or till gelatin starts to thicken; remove any remaining ice cubes. Fold in chopped apple, celery, and walnuts. Spoon mixture into 6 individual molds. Place in freezer for 20 minutes or till firm. Makes 6 servings.

Quick Waldorf Salad

35 MINUTES

Use 1 cup fresh seedless green grapes when they are in season –

- 1 4-ounce container whipped cream cheese
- ¼ cup milk
- 1 tablespoon lemon juice
- ½ teaspoon sugar
- 2 medium apples, cored and sliced
- ½ cup pitted whole dates, halved lengthwise
- 1 8¼-ounce can seedless grapes, drained
- ⅓ cup chopped walnuts
  Leaf lettuce

Thoroughly combine cream cheese, milk, lemon juice, and sugar. Stir in apples, dates, drained grapes, and walnuts. Cover; chill in freezer 20 minutes. Arrange fruit mixture on individual lettuce-lined plates. Serves 6.

Four-Fruit Salad

15 MINUTES

The buttermilk adds tartness to this creamy fruit salad –

- 1 8¼-ounce can crushed pineapple, chilled and drained
- ½ cup buttermilk
- 1 envelope vanilla instant breakfast mix
- 1 teaspoon lemon juice
  Several drops almond extract
- 1 16-ounce can peach slices, chilled and drained
- 1 16-ounce can pear halves, chilled, drained, and sliced
- 1 16-ounce can pitted light sweet cherries, chilled and drained

For dressing, in mixing bowl combine drained pineapple, buttermilk, dry vanilla breakfast mix, lemon juice, and almond extract; set aside.

In serving bowl combine chilled and drained peaches, pears, and sweet cherries; pour dressing over all. Makes 8 servings.

German Potato Salad

30 MINUTES

Canned potatoes take the work out of this saucy potato salad –

- 2 slices bacon
- 2 tablespoons sugar
- 1 tablespoon all-purpose flour
- ½ teaspoon salt
- ⅛ teaspoon pepper
- ½ cup water
- 3 tablespoons vinegar
- 2 tablespoons thinly sliced green onion
- 2 16-ounce cans sliced potatoes, drained
- ½ cup dairy sour cream
- 1 teaspoon dijon-style mustard

In skillet cook bacon till crisp. Drain bacon, reserving drippings in skillet. Crumble bacon; set aside. Stir sugar, flour, salt, and pepper into reserved drippings. Add water, vinegar, and onion. Cook and stir till mixture thickens and bubbles. Stir in drained potatoes; heat through. Remove from heat; blend in sour cream and mustard. Turn into serving bowl; sprinkle with bacon. Makes 4 to 6 servings.

Macaroni-Slaw Salad

35 MINUTES

A hint of lemon provides the tanginess –

- 2 15-ounce cans macaroni in cheese sauce, chilled
- ½ cup dairy sour cream
- 1 tablespoon prepared mustard
- 1 tablespoon lemon juice
- 1 teaspoon salad seasoning
- ½ teaspoon salt
- 2 6½- or 7-ounce cans tuna, drained and flaked
- 2 cups shredded cabbage
- ½ cup sliced pitted ripe olives

Cut up long pieces of macaroni, if necessary. In mixing bowl combine chilled canned macaroni in cheese sauce, sour cream, mustard, lemon juice, salad seasoning, and salt. Fold in tuna, shredded cabbage, and sliced olives. Chill in freezer 15 to 20 minutes. Serves 6.

SALADS

Basic Tossed Salad

30 MINUTES

- 6 cups torn iceberg lettuce, romaine, bibb lettuce, spinach, endive, or leaf lettuce
- 1 cup sliced carrot, celery, or radish
- ½ medium onion or red onion, cut into rings or ¼ cup sliced green onion
- 2 medium tomatoes, cut into wedges or 1 cup cherry tomatoes, halved

  Desired dressing (see recipes below and at right or use bottled salad dressing)

In large bowl mix any combination of 6 cups torn greens and one choice from each of the other ingredient options. Serve with choice of dressing. Serves 8.

Here are some easy ways to transform plain mayonnaise into a delicious salad dressing. To 1 cup **mayonnaise or salad dressing,** *stir in your choice of the seasoning combinations listed below.*
Poppy Seed Dressing: *Stir in ¼ cup* **sugar,** *2 tablespoons* **poppy seed,** *and 2 tablespoons* **lemon juice.** *Makes 1¼ cups.*
Chive Dressing: *Stir in ¼ cup snipped* **chives,** *1 tablespoon* **lemon juice,** *2 teaspoons* **tarragon vinegar,** *and dash* **salt.** *Makes about 1¼ cups.*
Blue Cheese Dressing: *Stir in ¼ cup crumbled* **blue cheese,** *3 to 4 tablespoons* **milk,** *and several dashes* **bottled hot pepper sauce.** *Makes about 1⅓ cups.*
Creamy Dressing: *Whip ½ cup* **whipping cream** *to soft peaks. Fold into mayonnaise. Makes 1¾ cups.*
Curry Dressing: *Stir in 2 to 3 tablespoons* **milk,** *1 tablespoon finely chopped* **chutney,** *and ½ teaspoon* **curry powder.** *Makes 1¼ cups.*

Mushroom Dressing

30 MINUTES

- 1 10¾-ounce can condensed cream of mushroom soup
- 1 thin slice onion
- ¼ cup grated parmesan cheese
- 2 tablespoons worcestershire sauce
- 2 tablespoons vinegar
- 1 teaspoon paprika
- ½ cup salad oil

  Basic Tossed Salad (see recipe, left)

In blender container combine soup (*do not* add water), onion, cheese, worcestershire, vinegar, paprika, and ⅛ teaspoon *pepper*; cover and blend on low speed till combined. Through hole in lid, or with lid slightly ajar, gradually add salad oil in thin steady stream. Cover; chill 15 minutes. Serve over Basic Tossed Salad. Makes 2 cups.

Grasshopper Parfaits

45 MINUTES

2 1½-ounce envelopes dessert
   topping mix
¾ cup milk
2 tablespoons green crème de
   menthe
1 tablespoon white crème de
   cacao
1 cup coarsely crumbled
   chocolate chip cookies

In mixing bowl combine first 4 ingredients; mix using low speed of electric mixer. Beat at high speed about 2 minutes or till soft peaks form; beat 2 minutes more. Layer mixture into parfait glasses, using about 2 tablespoons cookie crumbs between each layer. Top with a piece of crumbled cookie. Chill in freezer till serving time. Garnish with mint leaves, if desired. Serves 4.

Cherry-Brownie Bake

45 MINUTES

1 21-ounce can cherry pie filling
2 tablespoons lemon juice
2 tablespoons butter
1 8-ounce package brownie mix
   Vanilla ice cream

Preheat oven to 375°. In saucepan combine pie filling, lemon juice, butter, and ⅓ cup *water*. Bring to boiling, stirring to melt butter; keep warm. Meanwhile, prepare brownie mix according to package directions. Turn hot cherry mixture into a 12x7½x2-inch baking dish. Spoon brownie batter in 8 portions atop. Bake in 375° oven 30 to 35 minutes. Serve warm with ice cream. Serves 8.
Microwave Method: In a 12x7½x2-inch nonmetal baking dish mix pie filling, lemon juice, butter, and ⅓ cup *water*. Cook, uncovered, in countertop microwave oven on high power for 6 to 7 minutes or till bubbly; stir twice to melt butter. Meanwhile, prepare brownie mix according to package directions. Spoon batter in 8 portions atop hot mixture. Micro-cook, uncovered, 10 minutes, giving dish a quarter turn every 2 to 3 minutes. Serve as above.

Apricot Dessert

35 MINUTES

¼ cup butter or margarine
1 21-ounce can apricot pie filling
1 11-ounce can mandarin orange
   sections with pineapple tidbits
   or mandarin orange sections,
   drained
1 package (6) refrigerated biscuits
2 tablespoons sugar
¼ teaspoon ground cinnamon

Preheat oven to 400°. In saucepan melt butter. Remove 2 tablespoons; set aside. Stir pie filling and drained fruit into butter in saucepan. Bring to boiling, stirring often. Separate dough into 6 biscuits; cut each into 3 pieces. Pour *hot* filling into 1½-quart casserole. Dip biscuit pieces into remaining butter; arrange atop fruit. Mix sugar and cinnamon; sprinkle over biscuits. Bake in 400° oven 15 to 20 minutes. Serves 6 to 8.

Praline Cheese Cups

45 MINUTES

1 4-ounce container whipped
   cream cheese
¼ cup dairy sour cream
2 tablespoons sugar
½ teaspoon vanilla
4 cake dessert cups
¼ cup pecan halves
½ cup caramel ice cream topping
1 tablespoon brandy

Combine first 4 ingredients. With fork, remove small amount of center from each dessert cup. Fill centers with cheese mixture. Arrange pecans atop each. Chill in freezer 35 minutes. Before serving, heat together caramel topping and brandy. Spoon atop dessert cups. Garnish each with maraschino cherry, if desired. Makes 4 servings.

For a spectacular dessert finale, serve Grasshopper Parfaits, top left; Praline Cheese Cups, top right; or Apricot Dessert, bottom.

Gingerbread Shortcake

30 MINUTES

1 14½-ounce package gingerbread mix
½ cup packed brown sugar
2 tablespoons cornstarch
2 cups frozen blueberries
1 8¼-ounce can crushed pineapple, drained
2 tablespoons butter
2 tablespoons lemon juice

Preheat oven to 350°. Prepare gingerbread according to package directions, *except* bake in a 13x9x2-inch baking pan in 350° oven for 18 to 20 minutes or till done. Meanwhile, for fruit sauce combine brown sugar and cornstarch in saucepan; gradually blend in 1 cup *water*. Add blueberries. Cook and stir till thickened and bubbly. Stir in pineapple, butter, and lemon juice. Spoon sauce over squares of warm gingerbread. Serves 12.

Coconut-Walnut Cake

45 MINUTES

¼ cup dark corn syrup
3 tablespoons butter, melted
3 tablespoons brown sugar
¾ cup flaked coconut
½ cup chopped walnuts
1½ cups Homemade Biscuit Mix (see recipe, page 92) or packaged biscuit mix
½ cup sugar
½ cup orange juice
1 egg
2 tablespoons cooking oil
1 teaspoon vanilla

Preheat oven to 375°. Combine corn syrup, butter, and brown sugar. Spread in bottom of greased 9x9x2-inch baking pan. Sprinkle with coconut and nuts. In mixer bowl combine Biscuit Mix or packaged mix, sugar, orange juice, egg, oil, and vanilla. Beat on low speed of electric mixer ½ minute, scraping sides of bowl. Beat at medium speed 4 minutes more. Pour batter into pan. Bake in 375° oven 20 minutes or till done. Immediately invert onto serving plate. Serve warm. Makes 9 servings.

Chocolate Torte

45 MINUTES

1 frozen loaf pound cake
4 squares (4 ounces) semisweet chocolate
1 15-ounce container ricotta cheese (about 2 cups)
½ cup sugar
1½ teaspoons vanilla
6 tablespoons Amaretto, orange liqueur, or crème de cacao
1 cup sifted powdered sugar
2 tablespoons unsweetened cocoa powder
1 tablespoon butter or margarine, melted
2 to 3 tablespoons boiling water
2 tablespoons chopped walnuts

Remove pound cake from freezer; let stand at room temperature. Meanwhile, finely chop chocolate squares. In bowl combine chopped chocolate, ricotta cheese, sugar, and vanilla. Slice pound cake horizontally into 3 equal layers. Drizzle *2 tablespoons* of the liqueur over *one* side of each cake layer. Set aside 2 tablespoons of the cheese filling. Divide remaining cheese filling in *half*; spread mixture evenly on the liqueur side of *two* of the cake layers. Stack the cake layers with filling; top with remaining cake layer. In mixing bowl stir together powdered sugar and cocoa. Add melted butter; stir in enough boiling water to make of glazing consistency. Spoon mixture over torte. Dollop the reserved cheese mixture atop cake; sprinkle with walnuts. Chill in freezer till serving time. Makes 8 servings.

To slice unfrosted cake into even horizontal layers, *just measure the desired height with a ruler and insert wooden picks as markers around the cake. Then use a sharp, long-bladed knife to slice through the cake using the picks as a guide.*

Few desserts are as tempting as Chocolate Torte. Within 45 minutes, you can enjoy this luscious dessert flavored with ricotta cheese, chocolate, and liqueur.

DESSERTS

Mock Cheesecake

15 MINUTES

Try using blueberry, apple, or pineapple pie filling, too—

1 frozen loaf pound cake
1 4-ounce container whipped cream cheese
1 21-ounce can cherry pie filling

Cut frozen cake into 8 individual slices. Spread one side of *each* slice with cream cheese. Place cake slices, cheese side up, on serving plates. Spoon about ¼ cup cherry pie filling over each. Makes 8 servings.

Spiced Fruit Compote

30 MINUTES

If you don't have coconut on hand, try coarsely crumbling your favorite cookie to serve on top of the fruit—

1 11-ounce package mixed dried fruits
3 cups water
2 tablespoons sugar
1 teaspoon cornstarch
1 teaspoon finely shredded lemon peel
½ teaspoon ground cinnamon
⅛ teaspoon ground nutmeg
¼ cup orange liqueur
1 tablespoon honey
Toasted coconut (optional)

Cut up any large pieces of fruit, if desired. In saucepan cook mixed fruits in the 3 cups water, covered, for 15 to 20 minutes or till done. Drain, reserving 1 cup fruit liquid. Set fruit aside. In saucepan stir together sugar, cornstarch, lemon peel, cinnamon, and nutmeg. Add reserved fruit liquid, orange liqueur, and honey. Cook and stir till thickened and bubbly. Stir in cooked fruit. Turn into serving dish or individual dessert dishes. Top with toasted coconut, if desired. Makes 6 servings.

Glazed Stuffed Apples

35 MINUTES

4 medium cooking apples, cored and halved
½ cup light raisins
¼ cup chopped walnuts
1 cup orange juice
¼ cup honey
¼ teaspoon ground nutmeg

Peel apples, if desired. Place apple halves, cut side up, in a 10-inch skillet. Fill apples with a mixture of raisins and walnuts. For glaze, combine orange juice, honey, and nutmeg. Pour mixture over and around apples. Bring to boiling; reduce heat. Simmer, covered, about 10 minutes or till tender. Uncover and simmer 10 minutes more, basting apples occasionally with glaze. Makes 8 servings.

Angel Fruit Dessert

35 MINUTES

This fancy dessert will remind you of a summertime shortcake. Try using the same flavors of fruit and yogurt one time, then mix flavors the next—

1 10-ounce package frozen strawberries, raspberries, blueberries, or peaches
½ cup whipping cream
¼ cup sugar
1 cup strawberry, raspberry, blueberry, or peach yogurt
3 cups angel cake cut into 1-inch cubes

Place choice of frozen fruit in carton in a bowl of warm water; set aside to thaw. Meanwhile, in mixer bowl beat whipping cream and sugar with rotary beater or electric mixer till soft peaks form. Fold in choice of yogurt. Fold in angel cake cubes. Turn cake mixture into an 11x7x2-inch pan. Cover; chill in freezer 20 minutes. To serve, spoon cake mixture into dessert dishes. Spoon some of the thawed fruit with syrup atop each serving. Serves 6.

Pronto Shortcakes

30 MINUTES

For four servings, use only one can of fruit and halve the sour cream mixture. Save the remaining rolls to reheat another time –

- 1 package (8) refrigerated cinnamon rolls with icing
- 1 cup dairy sour cream
- 2 tablespoons sugar
- 1 cup whipping cream
- 2 16-ounce cans peach slices or fruit cocktail

Preheat oven to 375°. Bake cinnamon rolls according to package directions. (Reserve icing for another use.) Meanwhile, blend together sour cream and sugar. Whip cream; fold into sour cream mixture. While still warm, split rolls in half crosswise with fork. Drain fruit, reserving 2 tablespoons syrup; drizzle reserved syrup over roll halves. Spoon cream mixture and fruit between layers and over top. Makes 8 servings.

Peanut-Peach Cobbler

45 MINUTES

Save time by cutting the cookie dough into pieces with kitchen shears –

- ⅓ cup peanut butter
- ¼ cup packed brown sugar
- ¼ cup butter *or* margarine
- 1 tablespoon lemon juice
- 1 29-ounce can peach slices
- ½ roll refrigerated sugar cookie dough
  Vanilla ice cream

Preheat oven to 400°. In saucepan combine peanut butter, brown sugar, butter or margarine, and lemon juice. Heat and stir till smooth. Add *undrained* peaches, cutting up any large pieces. Heat till bubbly, stirring frequently. Meanwhile, cut cookie dough into 9 pieces. Turn *hot* peach mixture into an 8x8x2-inch baking dish. Immediately top with cookie dough pieces. Bake in 400° oven 25 minutes or till golden. Serve with ice cream. Makes 9 servings.

Apple-Date Dessert

45 MINUTES

- 2 21-ounce cans apple pie filling
- ½ cup orange juice
- 1 14-ounce package date bar mix
- 1 beaten egg
- ½ cup chopped walnuts

Preheat oven to 375°. In saucepan heat together apple pie filling and orange juice till bubbly; keep warm. Meanwhile, prepare date filling from date bar mix according to package directions; stir in egg and nuts. Add the dry crumbly mixture from date mix; mix well. Pour *hot* apple mixture into a 12x7½x2-inch baking dish. Spoon date mixture in 8 portions atop apple filling. Bake in 375° oven about 30 minutes. Serve warm. Serves 8.

Microwave Method: Combine pie filling and orange juice in a 12x7½x2-inch nonmetal baking dish. Cook, uncovered, in countertop microwave oven on high power 10 minutes or till bubbly, stirring twice. Meanwhile, prepare date topper as above; spoon over apples in 8 portions. Micro-cook, uncovered, 10 minutes or till done, giving dish a quarter turn every 3 minutes.

Ginger Cupcakes

35 MINUTES

- 1 8¼-ounce can crushed pineapple
- 3 tablespoons butter
- ½ cup packed brown sugar
- 1 14-ounce package gingerbread mix

Preheat oven to 400°. Drain pineapple, reserving syrup. In small saucepan melt butter. Remove from heat; stir in brown sugar and the drained pineapple. Spoon into 18 muffin cups. Prepare gingerbread mix according to package directions *except* use pineapple syrup plus enough water to equal liquid called for in package directions. Divide batter between muffin cups, filling ⅔ full (do not overfill pans). Bake in 400° oven 15 minutes. Let cool 5 minutes. Loosen and invert onto wire rack. Serve warm. Makes 18.

Orange-Eggnog Frappé

10 MINUTES

- 2 cups dairy eggnog
- ⅓ cup orange liqueur
- 3 tablespoons frozen orange juice concentrate
- 1 pint vanilla ice cream
  Ground nutmeg

Combine eggnog, orange liqueur, and frozen orange concentrate. Stir to melt concentrate. Scoop ice cream into 4 tall glasses; pour eggnog mixture over ice cream. Muddle mixture slightly with spoon. Sprinkle nutmeg over each serving. Makes 4 (6-ounce) servings.

Banana-Lemon Shake

10 MINUTES

- 1 cup milk
- ½ of a 6-ounce can (⅓ cup) frozen lemonade concentrate
- 2 small bananas, cut up
- 1 pint vanilla ice cream

In blender container mix first 3 ingredients. Cover; blend till smooth. Add ice cream. Cover; blend till smooth. Makes 3 (8-ounce) servings.

Honey-Peanut Sipper

10 MINUTES

- 2 cups milk
- ¼ cup creamy peanut butter
- 1 tablespoon honey
- 4 marshmallows

In blender container combine first 3 ingredients. Cover and blend till smooth. Pour into saucepan; heat till *almost* boiling, stirring occasionally. *Do not boil.* Pour into mugs. Top with marshmallows. Makes 4 (5-ounce) servings.
Microwave Method: Blend ingredients as above *except* pour into a 4-cup glass measure. Cook, uncovered, in countertop microwave oven on high power 3 to 4 minutes or till hot, but *not boiling*, stirring once. Serve as above.

Island Fruit Punch

15 MINUTES
Lemon or orange sherbet works well in this punch, too—

- 1 29-ounce can pear halves, chilled
- 1 12-ounce can frozen lemonade concentrate
- 3 cups unsweetened pineapple juice, chilled
- 1 28-ounce bottle (3½ cups) lemon-lime carbonated beverage, chilled
- 1 quart pineapple sherbet

Place *undrained* pears and frozen lemonade in blender container. Cover; blend till smooth. Combine with pineapple juice and 2 cups *cold water*. Pour about ¾ cup fruit mixture into each glass. Slowly add carbonated beverage, pouring down side of glass and leaving 2 inches at top. Top each with a sherbet scoop. Makes 10 (12-ounce) servings.

Mocha Milk Punch

10 MINUTES
Serve this sundae-in-a-glass after a hearty meal—

- 1 quart coffee ice cream
- 1 cup milk or light cream
- ¼ to ⅓ cup bourbon or light rum
- ¼ cup crème de cacao

In blender container combine *half* the ice cream, the milk or cream, bourbon or rum, and crème de cacao. Cover and blend till smooth. Pour into 6 glasses. Top with scoop of remaining ice cream. Garnish with chocolate curls, if desired. Makes 6 (6-ounce) servings.

Any meal goes better when you include a refreshing appetizer or dessert drink. To start off a meal, pour fruity Wine Welcomer from a pitcher, back (see recipe, page 81). And for dessert, serve tall frothy glasses of Island Fruit Punch, front left, or individual chocolate-topped servings of Mocha Milk Punch, front right.

Orange-Spiced Cocoa

15 MINUTES

⅓ cup sugar
⅓ cup unsweetened cocoa powder
4 inches stick cinnamon
4 whole cloves
1 teaspoon finely shredded orange peel
Dash salt
4 cups milk

In saucepan combine first 6 ingredients; stir in ½ cup *water*. Bring to boiling, stirring constantly; boil 1 minute. Stir in milk; heat *almost* to boiling. Remove spices; beat cocoa with rotary beater till foamy. Makes 6 (6-ounce) servings.

Yogurt-Fruit Fizz

10 MINUTES

2 cups raspberry, strawberry, *or* peach yogurt
1 10-ounce package frozen raspberries *or* sliced strawberries *or* peaches
Sugar *and* milk (optional)

Place yogurt and fruit in blender container. Cover; blend till foamy. Add sugar to sweeten and milk to thin, if desired. Makes 4 (6-ounce) servings.

Black Russian Eggnog

20 MINUTES

2 beaten eggs
1 cup milk
1 cup light cream
¼ cup coffee liqueur
2 tablespoons bourbon *or* vodka
2 teaspoons sugar
1 teaspoon instant coffee crystals

In saucepan mix all ingredients. Cook and stir 10 minutes or till mixture coats metal spoon. Pour into 6 cups. Sprinkle with ground coriander, if desired. Makes 6 (4-ounce) servings.

Choco-Peanut Floats

10 MINUTES

4 cups chocolate milk
⅓ to ½ cup creamy peanut butter
1 tablespoon vanilla
1 pint vanilla ice cream

In blender container place *2 cups* of the milk and the peanut butter. Cover; blend till smooth. Stir in remaining milk and vanilla. Pour into 4 tall glasses; add a scoop of ice cream to each. Makes 4 (8-ounce) servings.

Dessert Chocolate

10 MINUTES

1 envelope instant cocoa mix
¾ cup milk
2 tablespoons orange liqueur, coffee liqueur, apricot brandy, cherry brandy, *or* crème de cacao
Frozen whipped dessert topping

In saucepan combine cocoa mix and milk; heat through. Stir in desired liqueur or brandy. Pour into cups. Top with a dollop of whipped topping. Makes 2 (4-ounce) servings.

A cup of hot coffee for dessert makes *a delicious ending to any meal. Stir one of these* **seasoning variations** *into 1 teaspoon* **instant coffee crystals** *in a coffee cup. (If using brewed coffee, double the strength of the coffee.) Add ½ cup* **boiling water;** *stir. Top with* **whipped cream.** *Makes 1 (6-ounce) serving.*
Café Israel; *2 tablespoons* **chocolate-flavored syrup** *and 2 tablespoons* **orange liqueur.**
Café Columbian: *2 tablespoons* **coffee liqueur** *and 1 tablespoon* **chocolate-flavored syrup.**
Irish Coffee: *1 tablespoon* **Irish whiskey** *and 2 teaspoons* **sugar.**

Pineapple Sundae

30 MINUTES

2 cups diced fresh pineapple
⅓ cup kirsch or cherry brandy
⅓ cup orange juice
1 tablespoon sugar
  Vanilla ice cream

Combine diced fresh pineapple, kirsch or brandy, orange juice, and sugar. Cover and marinate in freezer 20 minutes. To serve, spoon fruit mixture over ice cream. Top with whipped cream, if desired. Serves 6 to 8.

Berry-Lemon Sauce

45 MINUTES
Serve over wedges of angel cake –

1 21-ounce can lemon pie filling
1 15-ounce can blueberries
2 tablespoons lemon juice

In mixing bowl combine lemon pie filling, *undrained* blueberries, and lemon juice. Chill in freezer about 35 minutes. Cover; store remaining sauce in refrigerator. Makes 4 cups sauce.

Mocha-Mallow Sauce

10 MINUTES

2 teaspoons instant coffee crystals
½ cup milk
1 can chocolate or butter pecan frosting
1 7-ounce jar marshmallow topping
  Vanilla ice cream

In 1-cup liquid measure dissolve coffee crystals in ¼ cup *hot water*. Stir in milk. In mixing bowl stir together frosting and the milk mixture. Stir in marshmallow topping. Drizzle over scoops of ice cream. Cover; store remaining sauce in refrigerator. Makes 3 cups.

Butterscotch Sauce

10 MINUTES
Next time you may want to substitute peanuts or toasted pecans for the cashews –

½ cup packed brown sugar
1 tablespoon cornstarch
¾ cup water
1 tablespoon butter or margarine
¼ cup broken cashews
  Vanilla ice cream

In 1-quart saucepan stir together brown sugar and cornstarch. Add water. Cook and stir over medium-high heat for 4 to 5 minutes or till thickened and bubbly. Stir in butter or margarine till melted; stir in cashews. Drizzle warm sauce over scoops of ice cream. Makes about 1¼ cups sauce.

Peach-Rum Sauce

15 MINUTES
Use to top plain pound cake, too –

1 16-ounce can peach slices
2 tablespoons sugar
2 teaspoons cornstarch
½ teaspoon instant coffee crystals
1 tablespoon rum
  Vanilla ice cream

Drain peaches, reserving ½ cup fruit syrup. Chop peaches; set aside. In small saucepan combine sugar, cornstarch, and coffee crystals; stir in reserved syrup. Cook and stir till thickened and bubbly. Stir in peaches; heat through. Remove from heat; stir in rum. Serve warm sauce over scoops of ice cream. Cover; store remaining sauce in refrigerator. Reheat to serve. Makes 1¾ cups sauce.
Microwave Method: Drain and chop peaches as above, reserving syrup. Meanwhile, in 2-cup glass measure combine sugar, cornstarch, and coffee crystals; stir in reserved syrup. Cook, uncovered, in countertop microwave oven on high power 3 to 4 minutes or till thickened and bubbly, stirring every minute. Stir in peaches. Micro-cook 1 minute more. Serve as above.

DESSERTS

Dessert Omelet

This omelet will work well for main-dish fillings, too—

- 3 eggs
- 2 tablespoons water
- ¼ teaspoon salt
- 2 tablespoons butter or margarine

• • •

Desired Omelet Variation (see recipes at right)

In mixing bowl beat together eggs, water, and salt with a fork till blended but not frothy.

In 8-inch skillet or omelet pan, heat butter or margarine till it sizzles and browns slightly. Lift and tilt pan to coat sides. Add egg mixture; cook over medium heat. As egg sets, run a spatula around edge of skillet, lifting egg to allow uncooked portion to flow underneath. When eggs are set but still shiny, remove from heat.

Spoon filling across center as indicated in desired omelet variation. Fold one-third of omelet over center. Overlap remaining third atop. Slide omelet to edge of pan. Tilt skillet and slide omelet out onto warm serving plate. Garnish with topper as indicated with desired variation. Makes 2 servings.

Fruit Omelet (15 MINUTES): Fill Dessert Omelet with ⅓ cup **raspberry, strawberry, blueberry, or peach yogurt.** Top omelet with ¾ cup fresh **raspberries, halved strawberries, blueberries,** or sliced **peaches** mixed with 2 tablespoons **sugar.**

Jam Omelet (15 MINUTES): Fill Dessert Omelet with mixture of ¼ cup desired **jam or preserves** and 2 teaspoons **lemon juice.** Sprinkle top with sifted **powdered sugar** and chopped **walnuts.**

Banana Omelet (20 MINUTES): Before preparing Dessert Omelet melt 2 tablespoons **butter or margarine** in saucepan. Stir in 2 tablespoons **brown sugar** and several dashes ground **cinnamon.** Cook and stir two or three minutes. Stir in 1 medium **banana,** sliced; heat through. Keep warm. Prepare Dessert Omelet. Fill with 2 tablespoons sifted **powdered sugar.** Serve banana-sugar mixture atop.

Cream Cheese Omelet (15 MINUTES): Fill Dessert Omelet with a mixture of ½ of a 4-ounce container **whipped cream cheese** and 1 tablespoon desired **jam or jelly.** Sprinkle top of omelet with sifted **powdered sugar.**

Sour Cream Omelet (15 MINUTES): Fill Dessert Omelet with ¼ cup dairy **sour cream.** Drizzle omelet with some **strawberry, pineapple, or butterscotch ice cream topping.**

Applesauce Omelet (15 MINUTES): In saucepan heat ½ cup chunk-style **applesauce** with ⅛ teaspoon ground **cinnamon or nutmeg;** use to fill Dessert Omelet. Top with a dollop of dairy **sour cream.**

Novelty Nachos

15 MINUTES

This snack gives you a choice of crackers or chips, toppers, and cheese –

2 cups crackers, tortilla chips, king-size corn chips, or melba toast

2 tablespoons canned green chili peppers, rinsed, seeded, and chopped; ½ cup sliced olives; ½ cup sliced mushrooms; ½ cup tiny canned shrimp; *and/or* ½ cup cooked bacon pieces

1 cup shredded cheddar, Swiss, muenster, monterey jack, or mozzarella cheese

Preheat broiler. Place a single layer of crackers or chips on baking sheet. Top with your choice of bite-size toppers. Sprinkle cheese over all. Broil 4 to 5 inches from heat about 1½ minutes or till cheese melts. Slide onto serving platter. Serve hot. Makes 4 to 6 servings.

Saucy Ham Nibbles

35 MINUTES

1 slightly beaten egg

¾ cup soft bread crumbs (1 slice bread)

1 teaspoon dry mustard

2 6¾-ounce cans chunked ham, drained and flaked

2 tablespoons cooking oil

1 cup cranberry-orange relish

½ cup dry white wine

2 tablespoons dried parsley flakes

2 teaspoons worcestershire sauce

In bowl combine egg, bread crumbs, and mustard. Add ham; mix well. Shape into 1-inch balls. In skillet quickly brown balls in hot oil. Combine cranberry-orange relish, wine, parsley flakes, and worcestershire sauce. Pour over ham balls; cover and simmer 10 minutes or till hot. Transfer to chafing dish; place over burner. Serve warm with wooden picks. Makes 3 dozen.

Beer-Sauced Links

20 MINUTES

2 pounds fully cooked Polish sausage or frankfurters, cut into ½-inch pieces

1 cup beer

¼ cup packed brown sugar

2 tablespoons cornstarch

¼ cup vinegar

¼ cup prepared mustard

1 tablespoon prepared horseradish

In skillet combine sausage and beer. Cover; simmer 10 minutes. Combine brown sugar and cornstarch. Stir in vinegar, mustard, and horseradish. Add to sausages; cook and stir till bubbly. Turn into fondue pot; place over fondue burner. Serve warm with wooden picks. Makes 36 pieces.

Spicy Sausage Bites

20 MINUTES

2 8-ounce packages brown-and-serve sausage links

1 15½-ounce jar meatless spaghetti sauce

1 tablespoon brown sugar

1 tablespoon vinegar

1½ teaspoons Italian or Mexican Seasoning Mix (see recipes, page 90)

1 6-ounce can whole mushrooms, drained

Cut sausages crosswise into thirds. In 10-inch skillet brown sausages; drain well. Add spaghetti sauce, brown sugar, vinegar, and Italian or Mexican Seasoning. Stir in drained mushrooms. Bring to boiling; reduce heat. Simmer, covered, 5 minutes. Turn into fondue pot; place over fondue burner. Serve warm with wooden picks. Makes 60.

Start off your next dinner or cocktail party with this lavish spread of appetizers that features Italian Tuna Dip with vegetable dippers, top left (see recipe, page 82); Beer-Sauced Links, top right; and Novelty Nachos, bottom.

Prairie Fire Dip

15 MINUTES

1 10¾-ounce can enchilada dip
½ cup shredded provolone cheese
  (2 ounces)
¼ cup milk
2 tablespoons butter or margarine
1 teaspoon minced dried onion
  Corn chips, tortilla chips, or
  vegetable dippers

In saucepan combine enchilada dip, cheese, milk, butter or margarine, and onion. Heat and stir for 5 to 10 minutes or till hot. Transfer dip to small fondue pot; place over fondue burner. Serve warm with chips or vegetable dippers. Makes 1¾ cups dip.

Microwave Method: In 2-cup glass measure combine dip, cheese, milk, butter or margarine, and onion. Cook in countertop microwave oven on high power for 3 minutes, stirring every minute. Serve as above.

Oriental Meatballs

45 MINUTES

2 cups soft bread crumbs
½ cup finely chopped water
  chestnuts
½ cup milk
2 tablespoons Oriental Seasoning
  (see recipe, page 89)
¼ teaspoon crushed red pepper
1 pound lean ground beef
  Bottled plum sauce, bottled
  sweet-sour sauce, or Hot
  Mustard Sauce (see recipe
  below)

Preheat oven to 350°. In a bowl combine bread crumbs, water chestnuts, milk, Oriental Seasoning, and red pepper. Add ground beef; mix well. Form into 1-inch balls. Place in a 15x10x1-inch baking pan. Bake in 350° oven 18 to 20 minutes. Serve with plum sauce, sweet-sour sauce, or Hot Mustard Sauce. Makes about 60 meatballs.

Hot Mustard Sauce: Combine ¼ cup *dry mustard*, 2 teaspoons *cooking oil*, and ½ teaspoon *salt*. Stir in ¼ cup *warm water*. Makes ⅓ cup sauce.

Crab Fondue

15 MINUTES

1 8-ounce package cream cheese
1 5-ounce jar American cheese
  spread
1 7½-ounce can crab, drained,
  flaked, and cartilage removed
2 tablespoons milk
2 tablespoons dry white wine
2 teaspoons worcestershire sauce
  French bread, cut into bite-size
  pieces

In saucepan over low heat melt together cream cheese and American cheese spread, stirring constantly. Stir in crab, milk, wine, and worcestershire sauce. Heat through. Transfer to fondue pot or chafing dish; place over burner. Serve with bread pieces. Makes 2¼ cups.

Microwave Method: In 4-cup glass measure, cook cream cheese and American cheese spread in counterop microwave oven on high power for 2 minutes, stirring every 30 seconds. Stir in crab, milk, wine, and worcestershire sauce. Micro-cook 3 minutes more, stirring after 1½ minutes. Serve as above.

Peppy Cocktail Nuts

30 MINUTES

¼ cup butter or margarine
1 tablespoon worcestershire sauce
½ teaspoon bottled hot pepper
  sauce
1 tablespoon salad seasoning
1 teaspoon salt
¼ teaspoon garlic salt
1 pound whole almonds, unsalted
  cashews, Brazil nuts, filberts,
  or peanuts

In 12-inch skillet with tight-fitting lid mix butter or margarine, worcestershire sauce, hot pepper sauce, salad seasoning, salt, garlic salt, and ¼ teaspoon *pepper*. Stir over low heat till butter melts and ingredients are blended. Add nuts, tossing to coat. Cook, covered, over low heat 20 minutes, stirring often. Cool 5 minutes on paper toweling. Store in airtight container. Makes 4½ cups.

Apple-Apricot Mix

15 MINUTES

⅓ cup sugar
12 inches stick cinnamon, broken up
½ teaspoon whole cloves
   Ice cubes
3 cups apple juice or cider, chilled
1 12-ounce can (1½ cups) apricot nectar, chilled
¼ cup lemon juice
   Vodka, brandy, rum, gin, white wine, or ginger ale

In small saucepan mix sugar, cinnamon, cloves, and ⅓ cup *water*. Bring to boiling. Cover; reduce heat. Simmer 10 minutes. Strain out spices; discard. Add *two* ice cubes to hot mixture. Mix apple juice, apricot nectar, and lemon juice. Stir in spiced mixture. To serve, pour 1 jigger desired liquor over ice in a glass. Add apple-apricot mix to taste; stir. Or, add mix to wine or ginger ale to taste. Makes 5 cups mix.
Microwave Method: In 2-cup glass measure mix sugar, cinnamon, cloves, and ⅓ cup *water*. Cook, uncovered, in countertop microwave oven on high power 3 minutes. Continue as above.

Wine Welcomer

15 MINUTES
This beverage is pictured on page 73 –

1 6-ounce can frozen lemonade concentrate
1 6-ounce can frozen orange juice concentrate
1 fifth dry white wine (750 ml)
1 cup orange liqueur
1 28-ounce bottle carbonated water
   Ice
   Orange slices (optional)

Place frozen concentrates in large pitcher or punch bowl. Gradually stir in 2 cups *cold water*, mixing till smooth. Stir in wine and orange liqueur. Add carbonated water and ice; stir gently. Top with orange slices, if desired. Serve at once. Makes 22 (4-ounce) servings.

Hot Spiced
Cranberry-Apple Wine

25 MINUTES

2 cups cranberry-apple drink
4 inches stick cinnamon, broken up
3 cardamom pods, shelled
2 cups port wine

In medium saucepan combine cranberry-apple drink, cinnamon, and cardamom. Simmer, uncovered, 10 minutes. Strain to remove spices. Stir in wine; heat through. Serve in mugs. Makes 4 (8-ounce) servings.
Microwave Method: In 4-cup glass measure combine cranberry-apple drink, cinnamon, and cardamom. Cook, uncovered, in countertop microwave oven on high power for 5 minutes. Strain to remove spices; return spiced mixture to glass measure. Stir in wine. Pour into four mugs. Micro-cook, uncovered, 2 minutes more or just till bubbly around edges, rearranging mugs once.

Hot Vegetable Sipper

15 MINUTES
If you enjoy spicy foods, add a dash of bottled hot pepper sauce –

2 12-ounce cans (3 cups) vegetable juice cocktail
2 teaspoons lemon juice
1 teaspoon worcestershire sauce
   Dried dillweed

In 1-quart saucepan combine vegetable juice cocktail, lemon juice, and worcestershire sauce. Heat, stirring occasionally, about 5 minutes or till bubbly. Pour into mugs. Sprinkle with dillweed. Makes 6 (4-ounce) servings.
Microwave Method: In 4-cup glass measure combine vegetable juice cocktail, lemon juice, and worcestershire sauce. Cook, uncovered, in countertop microwave oven on high power 3 minutes, stirring once. Pour into mugs. Sprinkle with dillweed.

Cranana Slush

15 MINUTES

1   6-ounce can frozen cranberry
    juice cocktail concentrate
¾   cup light rum
1   medium banana, broken up
2   tablespoons lemon juice
4   cups ice cubes

In blender container mix first four ingredients. Cover; blend till smooth. Add *half* the ice cubes; cover. Blend till smooth. Add remaining ice cubes. Cover; blend till slushy. Pour into glasses. Garnish with sliced banana, if desired. Makes 5 (6-ounce) servings.

Yogurt Sip

20 MINUTES

1   10-ounce package frozen peach
    slices
1   cup plain yogurt
¼   cup peach brandy or other
    brandy
¼   cup light rum
1   tablespoon honey
    Ground nutmeg

Let peaches stand at room temperature 10 minutes. Combine yogurt, brandy, rum, and honey in blender container. Add peaches and syrup. Cover; blend till smooth. Pour into glasses; top with nutmeg. Makes 5 (4-ounce) servings.

Frisky Sours

10 MINUTES

1   6-ounce can frozen
    grapefruit-orange juice
    concentrate
1   6-ounce can frozen lemonade
    concentrate
1½ cups whiskey
1½ cups cold water

In blender container combine all ingredients. Cover; blend just till mixed. Serve over ice, if desired. Makes 9 (4-ounce) servings.

Strawberry Spritzer

30 MINUTES

3   10-ounce packages frozen sliced
    strawberries
6   cups white grape juice
1   28-ounce bottle carbonated
    water, chilled
    Red food coloring (optional)

Let strawberries stand at room temperature 20 minutes. Place *two* of the packages of strawberries with their syrup in blender container. Cover and blend till smooth. In large pitcher or punch bowl combine blended strawberries, grape juice, and remaining package of berries. To serve, add carbonated water; stir. Add red food coloring, if desired. Makes 24 (4-ounce) servings.

Italian Tuna Dip

45 MINUTES
This tangy dip is shown on page 79 –

1   cup dairy sour cream
1   3¼- or 3½-ounce can tuna,
    drained and flaked
¼   cup grated parmesan cheese
1   tablespoon milk
2   teaspoons Italian salad dressing
    mix
1   teaspoon lemon juice
    Paprika
    Vegetable dippers

In small bowl combine sour cream, flaked tuna, parmesan cheese, milk, Italian salad dressing mix, and lemon juice. Cover; chill in freezer 30 minutes. Sprinkle with paprika. Serve with vegetable dippers. Makes 1½ cups dip.

Cool, refreshing fruit-flavored drinks are the perfect beginning to any meal. Serve Cranana Slush, left, a cranberry version of the daiquiri; Frisky Sours, center front, a whiskey sour with a touch of grapefruit; Strawberry Spritzer, center back, sliced frozen strawberries blended with white grape juice and carbonated water; or Yogurt Sip, right, a mixture of peach slices, yogurt, peach brandy, rum, and honey.

Beer-Cheese Dip

30 MINUTES

2 cups shredded cheddar cheese
 (8 ounces)
½ teaspoon prepared horseradish
¼ teaspoon dry mustard
⅛ teaspoon pepper
⅓ cup beer
2 tablespoons butter or margarine
 Vegetable dippers

In small mixer bowl combine cheese, horseradish, mustard, and pepper. In saucepan heat beer and butter or margarine just till butter melts and beer boils. Add to cheese mixture. Beat with electric mixer 4 to 5 minutes or till nearly smooth. Cool in freezer for 5 to 10 minutes. Serve with vegetable dippers. Makes 1½ cups dip.
Microwave Method: Prepare as above *except* combine beer and butter or margarine in 1-cup glass measure. Cook, uncovered, in countertop microwave oven on high power for 1 minute or till butter almost melts and beer boils. Assemble and serve as above.

Cheese-Pastrami Dip

15 MINUTES
Because blenders work differently, you may need from 1 to 3 tablespoons milk to achieve a mixture of dipping consistency –

1 3-ounce package sliced pastrami
1 8-ounce package cream cheese,
 cubed
1 small onion
1 to 3 tablespoons milk
¼ cup pitted ripe olives
 Assorted crackers

In blender container place pastrami. Cover; blend till shredded. Remove; set aside. To blender container add cream cheese and onion. Cover; blend till smooth. Blend in milk to desired consistency. Add olives; blend just till chopped. Turn into mixing bowl; stir in pastrami. Spoon into small bowl. Serve with crackers. Makes 1⅔ cups.

Tomato-Sour Cream Dip

40 MINUTES

1 cup dairy sour cream
1 single-serving envelope *instant*
 tomato soup mix
1 tablespoon milk
2 teaspoons lemon juice
1½ teaspoons worcestershire sauce
¼ teaspoon onion powder
 Several dashes bottled hot
 pepper sauce
 Vegetable dippers

In bowl combine all ingredients except vegetable dippers. Chill in freezer 30 minutes; serve with vegetable dippers. Makes 1 cup.

Blue Cheese Spread

25 MINUTES

1 8-ounce package cream cheese
1 4-ounce package blue cheese,
 crumbled
2 tablespoons milk
1 tablespoon anchovy paste
¼ teaspoon garlic powder
 Assorted crackers

Let cheeses stand at room temperature 15 minutes. Combine cheeses with remaining ingredients except crackers. Serve on crackers. Makes 1⅔ cups.

Peanut Butter Spread

20 MINUTES

½ of a 6-ounce can frozen orange
 juice concentrate
1 cup creamy peanut butter
1 cup dairy sour cream
 Apple wedges, firm banana
 slices, fresh pear spears, or
 toast triangles

Let juice concentrate stand at room temperature 10 minutes. In bowl mix peanut butter and sour cream. Stir in juice concentrate till smooth. Serve with fruit or toast. Makes 2¼ cups.

Three-Cheese Spread

25 MINUTES

Try this spread with vegetables, too—

- 1 3-ounce package cream cheese
- ¼ cup mayonnaise or salad dressing
- 1 cup shredded Swiss cheese (4 ounces)
- 1 cup shredded American cheese (4 ounces)
- 2 tablespoons chopped pimiento
- 1 teaspoon worcestershire sauce
- ½ teaspoon onion powder
- ¼ teaspoon bottled hot pepper sauce
  Crackers or bread rounds

In small mixer bowl beat together cream cheese and mayonnaise or salad dressing; add Swiss and American cheeses. Beat with electric mixer for 3 to 5 minutes, scraping bowl often till well blended. Add pimiento, worcestershire sauce, onion powder, and pepper sauce. Serve as a spread on crackers or bread rounds. Makes 1⅔ cups.

Orange-Cheese Spread

35 MINUTES

This spread makes a good topping for warm apple pie—

- 2 cups shredded cheddar cheese (8 ounces)
- 1 4-ounce container whipped cream cheese
- 2 tablespoons butter or margarine
- ½ teaspoon finely shredded orange peel
- ¼ cup orange juice
- ¼ teaspoon dry mustard
  Fresh sliced fruit or assorted crackers

Place cheddar cheese, cream cheese, and butter in small mixer bowl; let stand at room temperature 20 minutes. Add orange peel, orange juice, and dry mustard. Beat with electric mixer till smooth and fluffy. Serve immediately on sliced fruit or crackers. Makes 2 cups.

Curry-Cheese Slices

30 MINUTES

- 2 3-ounce packages cream cheese
- 2 tablespoons milk
- 1 tablespoon dried parsley flakes
- 1 teaspoon curry powder
- ¼ cup chopped peanuts
  Party rye bread slices
- ¼ cup water
- 1 tablespoon lemon juice
  Thinly sliced apple wedges

Open cream cheese packages; let stand at room temperature 15 minutes. In a bowl combine cheese, milk, parsley flakes, and curry powder. Stir in peanuts. Spread on rye bread. In small bowl combine water and lemon juice. Dip apple wedges in lemon mixture. Place 1 wedge atop each sandwich. Makes 15 appetizer sandwiches.

Avocado-Cheese Rounds

25 MINUTES

- 1 large ripe avocado
- 2 teaspoons lemon juice
- 1 5-ounce jar cheese spread with bacon
  Party pumpernickel bread slices or assorted round crackers
  Chopped pimiento or snipped parsley

Pit and peel avocado; mash (mixture should measure about ¾ cup). In bowl stir lemon juice into mashed avocado. Spread about 1 level teaspoon cheese on bread rounds or crackers. Then spread 1 rounded teaspoon avocado mixture atop cheese. Garnish with pimiento or parsley. Serve at once. Makes 30 rounds.

***Crisp crackers are the perfect complement to dips and spreads.** To re-crisp crackers that have become a little soft, spread a single layer of crackers on a baking sheet and heat them in a 350° oven for 3 to 5 minutes.*

Make the Most of Your Time

Cooking nutritious appetizing meals quickly and without fuss is easy if you take a few minutes to get organized.

First, plan your meals for several days or a week at a time. If you choose the recipes for each of your meals (see the tips on menu planning below) and then compile one large grocery list, you'll eliminate any last-minute panic about what to serve and you'll also cut down on the number of trips you make to the store.

Next, arrange your kitchen so you can find what you need quickly. Store utensils you use often in easy-to-reach cupboards and drawers, and when possible, place ingredients in easy-to-open containers. Also, have duplicate measuring spoons and cups, mixing bowls, and mixing spoons so you won't have to take time to wash utensils in mid-recipe.

To avoid any unexpected snags, read your recipe thoroughly before you start. You'll also save time by assembling ingredients and utensils before you begin.

Finally, look for ways to "dovetail" preparation steps in a recipe. For example, when a recipe calls for both cooked rice and chopped celery, chop the celery while the rice is cooking.

Menu Planning

Try these simple guidelines for planning quick menus:
• Serve two- or three-course meals. Make at least one of these courses a simple food rather than a recipe—like lettuce with bottled dressing for a salad, or ice cream for dessert.
• Serve a variety of textures. If your main dish is a soft food, include a crisp salad as part of the meal.
• Balance flavors. Serve a tart food with a bland one. Watch seasonings carefully, and make sure that one flavor doesn't dominate the meal. Usually one highly seasoned food per menu is enough.
• Avoid serving foods that are all mixtures. For example, team a tossed vegetable salad with a piece of meat, fish, or poultry rather than with a casserole that's also a mixture of ingredients.
• Serve a balance of hot and cold foods, and be sure the foods are really hot or cold—not lukewarm.
• Fit your dessert to the rest of the meal. Serve a rich dessert with a light meal and vice versa.

Here are three menus for spur-of-the-moment meals. You'll find the page numbers for recipes marked with an asterisk (*) listed in the Index beginning on page 93.

Company Breakfast

Melon Wedges
*Cheese-Bacon Waffles**
Butter   *Maple Syrup*
*Orange-Spiced Cocoa**

When you have unexpected overnight guests, serve them this tempting breakfast menu.

Dinner for Six

*Ham-Vegetable Stew**
Lettuce Wedges
with
Green Goddess Dressing
*Quick Lemon Tarts**
Coffee

Try this easy-on-the-cook menu for your next dinner party. The stew has a biscuit topper, so there's no need to serve bread.

Impromptu Party

*Apricot-Apple Mix**
*Spicy Sausage Bites**
*Italian Tuna Dip**
Vegetable Dippers
Mixed Nuts

When the gang gets together after work to relax, let them munch on this selection of appetizers. For beverages, just make Apricot-Apple Mix and let your guests choose from vodka, brandy, rum, or gin to go with it.

Tips for Saving Time

You'll find the recipes in this book have been streamlined wherever possible to save you time. But you can speed up food preparation even more by using some of the following hints.

• Avoid the time-consuming chore of chopping onion and green pepper or mincing garlic by using commercially frozen chopped onion or green pepper, minced dried onion or garlic, onion powder, or garlic powder.

• If frozen chopped onion or green pepper is too much for your budget, chop and freeze your own. Seal the chopped onion or green pepper in plastic bags or freezer containers. Label and store in your freezer for up to a month.

• For a quick garnish or to use in recipes, chop nuts and toast them in a shallow baking pan in a 350° oven for 5 to 10 minutes or till browned, stirring once or twice. Cool the nuts in the pan, seal them in plastic bags or freezer containers, then label and freeze.

• Keep toasted coconut on hand to use in desserts or as a quick garnish. To toast coconut, place a thin layer in a shallow baking pan. Bake in a 350° oven for 6 to 8 minutes or till lightly browned, stirring once or twice. Cool coconut to room temperature. Then store in your refrigerator or in a plastic bag or freezer container in your freezer.

• Snip parsley quickly by placing the uncut parsley in a measuring cup and snipping it with kitchen shears.

• Shred American, cheddar, Swiss, or mozzarella cheese in batches to save time and effort. Plan your menus for two or three days ahead and shred the amount of cheese you'll need all at once. Seal it in plastic bags; then label and store in your refrigerator.

• Sift flour only when using cake flour (it has a tendency to pack down). For general baking, sifting all-purpose flour is an extra step. Just stir the all-purpose flour, spoon it lightly into a measuring cup, and level it off with a straight-edged knife. Never pack flour into the measuring cup.

• Measure stick butter or margarine the easy way by using the markings right on the wrapper. If your brand doesn't have the markings, just remember that one stick of butter or margarine is ½ cup, a half-stick is ¼ cup, and a quarter-stick is 2 tablespoons.

• Chill foods quickly by placing them in your freezer for 20 to 30 minutes.

• Keep a supply of hard-cooked eggs in your refrigerator to use in recipes. Hard-cooked eggs will remain fresh for up to one week in your refrigerator.

• Cut the cooking time of meat loaves by shaping them into individual round loaves in a baking pan, or by baking the meat mixture in muffin cups.

• Shape ground meat into patties. Place two pieces of waxed paper between each patty, then wrap, label, and freeze. The next time you need burgers in a hurry, they'll be already shaped and you can quickly remove just the number you need from the freezer. Individual patties thaw more quickly than 1-pound packages of ground meat, too.

• If making meatballs is a bother, here are two ways to make shaping them fast and simple. Shape the meat mixture into a log and cut off slices. These slices will roll easily into balls. Or, pat the meat into a square and cut it into cubes. The cubes also roll easily into even-sized meatballs.

• Don't take time to thaw frozen fish before broiling. You'll find you can cut the fish block into serving-size portions and broil it straight from the freezer in the same time it takes you to broil fresh fish.

• Shortcut salad making by serving wedges of lettuce rather than torn salad greens.

• Skip last-minute food preparation by making casseroles ahead. Most casseroles can be made and refrigerated up to 24 hours before cooking. Just add 15 to 20 minutes to the normal cooking time.

• Make gelatin salads in a hurry by spooning your favorite gelatin salad mixture into individual molds, custard cups, or plastic cups and chilling them in the freezer for 20 to 25 minutes.

• For biscuits on the double, use a drop biscuit recipe rather than kneading, rolling, and cutting regular biscuits.

• When you need a sauce on the spur of the moment, heat a can of undiluted condensed cream of mushroom, cream of celery, cream of chicken, cream of shrimp, cream of onion, cheddar cheese, or tomato soup.

• Slice a loaf of French bread to, but not through the bottom crust. Spread the cut edges with softened butter or garlic butter. Wrap the loaf in foil and label and freeze. Then when unexpected company arrives, simply heat the loaf in the oven in its foil wrapping.

- Freeze dollops of whipped cream to use with desserts. Whip the cream, then drop heaping spoonfuls onto a chilled baking sheet, swirling tops with a spoon. Freeze the dollops right on the baking sheet. When they're hard, remove them from the baking sheet with a spatula and place them in a plastic bag. Seal tightly, label, and freeze for up to three months. To use, place dollops atop dessert and let stand a few minutes to thaw.
- Grease and flour baking pans all in one step with pan coating. To make pan coating, thoroughly mix ½ cup *shortening* and ¼ cup *all-purpose flour*. Store extra coating in a covered container at room temperature.
- For quick lunches, make sandwiches ahead and freeze them for up to two weeks. You'll find the fillings that work best are those that use cream cheese, peanut butter, and sliced or ground cooked meat, poultry, or fish. Avoid freezing sandwiches with lettuce, celery, tomatoes, cucumbers, egg whites, jelly, or mayonnaise.

Use Appliances For Speed

While many of the time-saving appliances now available are not essential to preparing good meals in a hurry, they can be handy tools if you happen to own one or more of them.

Blender: Meal preparation can be a snap if you put your blender to work for you. Try using it to blend dry bread into fine dry bread crumbs, or fresh bread into soft bread crumbs. When you're making a vanilla wafer or graham cracker crust, the blender crushes the crackers or cookies in a flash. Take the work out of preparing fruit juice concentrates or dissolving gelatin by whirling them in the blender. It also makes quick and easy milk shakes and other beverages. Finally, the blender is great for combining salad dressings, pureeing vegetables and fruits, grating hard cheeses, and chopping cabbage for coleslaw.

Food Processor: While more elaborate than the blender, this appliance does many of the same chores in addition to other tasks such as shredding cheddar or Swiss cheese, slicing vegetables, and making peanut butter or almond paste. Also try using your food processor for chopping large quantities of nuts to store in the freezer or for blending meat loaf mixtures.

Countertop Oven Appliances: These handy portable ovens can be used indoors wherever there's an electrical outlet. What's more, they save time by heating up more quickly than your large regular oven, and they don't heat up the kitchen. For those times when speed is critical, use your countertop oven along with your range oven to prepare recipes with different baking temperatures at the same time.

Pressure Cooker: These saucepans help you cook foods in about one-third the normal time. The principle behind pressurized cooking is that steam under pressure raises the temperature of liquids higher than the boiling point of water and cooks food faster. Because of the short cooking time and the small amount of water used, cooking vegetables in a pressure cooker helps retain nutrients as well as color. Pressure cooking really saves time with normally slow cooking foods such as stews, pot roasts, or ribs.

Mixes to Make Ahead

Below and on the next three pages are ten timesaving mixes. If you take a few moments now to prepare these mixes, they'll save you a great deal of time on occasions when you have only a few minutes to get a meal on the table. **These mixes have been used in recipes throughout this book,** but you'll find them easy to adapt to your own family favorites, as well. What's even better is that they're often more economical than the commercial versions sold at the supermarket.

Oriental Seasoning

Use this seasoning as a marinade for burgers, steak, or chops—

- 1 cup soy sauce
- ⅓ cup light molasses
- 2 tablespoons ground ginger
- 2 tablespoons dry mustard
- 1 teaspoon garlic powder
- ½ teaspoon onion powder

In jar with screw-top lid combine soy sauce, molasses, ginger, mustard, garlic powder, and onion powder; shake to mix. Store, covered, in the refrigerator for up to six weeks. Makes 1⅓ cups.

See Index for recipes that use these mixes.

Italian Seasoning Mix

⅓ cup minced dried onion
3 tablespoons dried green pepper flakes
1 tablespoon instant beef bouillon granules
1 tablespoon dried basil
2 large bay leaves, crumbled or ½ teaspoon crushed bay leaves
2 teaspoons fennel seed
¼ teaspoon garlic powder

Combine onion, green pepper flakes, beef bouillon granules, basil, bay leaves, fennel seed, and garlic powder. Store in an airtight container. Shake or stir thoroughly to mix ingredients before measuring. Makes ⅔ cup mix.

Mexican Seasoning Mix

Use this mix to flavor chili or tacos –

⅓ cup minced dried onion
¼ cup dried parsley flakes
1 tablespoon instant chicken bouillon granules
1 tablespoon chili powder
2 teaspoons crushed red pepper
1 teaspoon dried oregano
¼ teaspoon garlic powder

Combine onion, parsley flakes, bouillon granules, chili powder, red pepper, oregano, and garlic powder. Store in an airtight container. Shake or stir thoroughly to mix ingredients before measuring. Makes ¾ cup mix.

***For a quick sandwich idea,** prepare either of the gravy recipes at right. Then spoon the gravy over heated slices of leftover cooked beef, pork, chicken, or turkey layered on top of toasted English muffin halves or thick slices of French bread.*

Beef Gravy Base

Serve Beef Gravy over roast beef, pork chops, or mashed potatoes –

1⅓ cups nonfat dry milk powder
¾ cup all-purpose flour
3 tablespoons instant beef bouillon granules
¼ teaspoon dried thyme, crushed
½ cup butter or margarine
2 teaspoons Kitchen Bouquet

Combine dry milk powder, flour, bouillon granules, and thyme. Cut in butter or margarine and Kitchen Bouquet till pieces resemble cornmeal. Store in tightly covered container in refrigerator up to two months. Makes about 3 cups (enough for 6 cups gravy).
   Beef Gravy (10 minutes): In saucepan slowly blend 1 cup *cold water* into ½ cup *Beef Gravy Base.* Cook and stir till mixture is thickened and bubbly. Cook 1 minute more. Makes 1 cup.

Chicken Gravy Base

Serve Chicken Gravy over roast chicken or turkey and dressing –

1⅓ cups nonfat dry milk powder
¾ cup all-purpose flour
3 tablespoons instant chicken bouillon granules
¼ teaspoon ground sage
½ cup butter or margarine
⅛ teaspoon yellow food coloring

Combine dry milk powder, flour, chicken bouillon granules, and sage. Cut in butter or margarine and food coloring till pieces resemble cornmeal. Store in tightly covered container in refrigerator up to two months. Makes about 3 cups (enough for 6 cups gravy).
   Chicken Gravy (10 minutes): In saucepan blend 1 cup *cold water* into ½ cup *Chicken Gravy Base.* Cook and stir till mixture is thickened and bubbly. Cook 1 minute more. Makes 1 cup.

Frozen Pizza Crust

This crust gives you last-minute convenience as well as homemade yeast bread flavor –

- 5½ to 6 cups all-purpose flour
- 2 packages active dry yeast
- 2 teaspoons salt
- 2 cups warm water (110° to 115°)
- 2 tablespoons cooking oil

In large mixer bowl stir together 2½ cups of the flour, the yeast, and salt; add warm water and oil. Beat on low speed of electric mixer ½ minute, scraping sides of bowl constantly. Beat 3 minutes at high speed.

By hand, stir in as much of the remaining flour as you can mix in with a spoon. On a lightly floured surface, knead in enough of the remaining flour to make a stiff dough. Continue kneading about 10 minutes or till dough is smooth and elastic (dough should be firm). Place in greased bowl, turning once to grease surface. Cover; let rise in a warm place 1½ to 2 hours or till more than double. Punch down, divide into fourths. Cover; let rest 10 minutes.

Preheat oven to 400°. On lightly floured surface roll each fourth to a 12-inch circle. Place each on greased 12-inch pizza pan, pressing to form edges on crust (or make rectangular pizzas on a baking sheet). Shape 4 pieces of heavy-duty foil into 11½-inch circles and place atop each crust to keep crust from rising. Bake pizza crusts, two at a time, in 400° oven for 12 minutes, removing foil during last 5 minutes of baking (crust will not be brown). Remove from oven; cool in pans on wire rack. Remove from pans; wrap each in foil. Label and freeze. Makes 4 crusts.

To use crust, return crust to pizza pan; top frozen crust with your favorite pizza sauce and toppers. Bake in 425° oven 20 to 25 minutes.

For ease in getting yeast breads to rise, *proof them in your unheated oven. It provides a warm draft-free place to set your bowl of dough. Place dough on the upper rack, and a bowl of hot water on the lower rack. Keep oven door closed so the heat from the water stays inside.*

Freezer Meatballs

Use these meatballs in soups or with bottled spaghetti sauce over pasta –

- 4 beaten eggs
- 1½ cups milk
- 1 cup fine dry bread crumbs*
- ½ cup finely chopped onion
- ¼ cup snipped parsley
- 2 teaspoons salt
- 1 teaspoon dried thyme, crushed
- ¼ teaspoon pepper
- 3 pounds ground beef

Preheat oven to 350°. In large bowl, combine eggs, milk, bread crumbs, onion, parsley, salt, thyme, and pepper. Add ground beef. Mix well. Shape into sixty 1½-inch meatballs. Place on two 15x10x1-inch baking pans. Bake in 350° oven 30 minutes. Drain on paper toweling. Cool. Wrap in three 20-meatball packages. Freeze up to six months. Makes 60 meatballs or 12 servings.

Corn Bread Mix

- 5 cups yellow cornmeal
- 4½ cups all-purpose flour
- 2 cups nonfat dry milk powder
- 1¼ cups sugar
- ⅓ cup baking powder
- 1 tablespoon salt
- 1¼ cups shortening that does not require refrigeration

In large bowl combine cornmeal, flour, nonfat dry milk powder, sugar, baking powder, and salt. Cut in shortening till mixture resembles coarse crumbs. Store in a covered airtight container up to six weeks. Stir mix lightly before measuring. To use, spoon mix lightly into measuring cup; level off with straight-edged knife. Makes 15 cups.

Corn Bread (35 minutes): Preheat oven to 425°. Stir *Corn Bread Mix* thoroughly. Measure 2½ cups mix; place in a bowl. Beat together 2 eggs and 1 cup *water* or *milk* with a rotary beater. Add to mix; beat with rotary beater till just smooth. Pour into greased 9x9x2-inch baking pan. Bake in 425° oven for 20 to 25 minutes.

Homemade Biscuit Mix

- 10 cups all-purpose flour
- ⅓ cup baking powder
- ¼ cup sugar
- 4 teaspoons salt
- 2 cups shortening that does not require refrigeration

In large mixing bowl stir together flour, baking powder, sugar, and salt. With pastry blender, cut in shortening till mixture resembles coarse crumbs. Store in covered airtight container up to six weeks at room temperature. To use, spoon mix lightly into measuring cup; level off with straight-edged knife. (For longer storage, place in a sealed freezer container and store in the freezer for up to six months. To use, allow mix to come to room temperature.) Makes 12½ cups.

Pancakes (20 minutes): In a bowl combine 2 beaten *eggs* and 1 cup *milk.* Add 2 cups *Homemade Biscuit Mix;* beat with rotary beater till nearly smooth. Cook pancakes on hot lightly greased griddle 2 to 3 minutes, turning once. Makes 10.

Biscuits (25 minutes): Preheat oven to 450°. Place 2 cups *Homemade Biscuit Mix* in a bowl; make a well. Add ½ cup *milk.* Stir with fork just till dough follows fork around bowl. On lightly floured surface knead dough 10 to 12 strokes. Roll or pat to ½-inch thickness. Cut dough with floured 2½-inch biscuit cutter. Bake on baking sheet in 450° oven 10 to 12 minutes. Makes 10.

Muffins (35 minutes): Preheat oven to 400°. Combine 3 cups *Homemade Biscuit Mix* and 3 tablespoons *sugar.* Mix 1 beaten *egg* and 1 cup *milk;* add all at once to dry ingredients. Stir just till moistened. Fill greased 2½-inch muffin pans ⅔ full. Bake in 400° oven for 20 to 25 minutes or till golden. Makes 12.

Avoid last-minute hassles by baking your muffins ahead and reheating them. To warm muffins, sprinkle them lightly with water and wrap in foil. Heat the muffins in a 400° oven for 15 to 20 minutes or till warm.

Whole Wheat-Honey
Biscuit Mix

- 8 cups all-purpose flour
- 2 cups whole wheat flour
- 1 cup dry buttermilk powder or nonfat dry milk powder
- ⅓ cup baking powder
- 1 tablespoon salt
- 2 cups shortening that does not require refrigeration
- • • •
- ¼ cup honey

In large mixing bowl thoroughly stir together all-purpose flour, whole wheat flour, buttermilk or nonfat dry milk powder, baking powder, and salt. With pastry blender, cut shortening into dry ingredients till mixture resembles coarse crumbs. Drizzle honey over flour mixture. Mix well. Store, covered, up to six weeks at room temperature. Before measuring, stir mix lightly. Spoon mix lightly into measuring cup; level off with straight-edged knife. (For longer storage, place in a sealed freezer container and store in freezer for up to six months. To use, allow mix to come to room temperature.) Makes 13½ cups mix.

Whole Wheat-Honey Pancakes (20 minutes): In a bowl combine 1 beaten *egg* and 1⅓ cups *milk.* Add 2 cups *Whole Wheat-Honey Biscuit Mix;* beat with rotary beater till nearly smooth. Cook pancakes on hot lightly greased griddle 2 to 3 minutes, turning once. Makes 10 pancakes.

Whole Wheat-Honey Biscuits (25 minutes): Preheat oven to 450°. Place 2 cups *Whole Wheat-Honey Biscuit Mix* in a bowl; add ½ cup *milk* all at once. Stir with fork just till dough follows fork around bowl. On lightly floured surface knead dough 10 to 12 strokes. Roll or pat to ½-inch thickness. Cut dough with floured 2½-inch biscuit cutter. Bake on baking sheet in 450° oven for 10 to 12 minutes. Makes 10 biscuits.

Whole Wheat-Honey Muffins (35 minutes): Preheat oven to 400°. In a bowl combine 3 cups *Whole Wheat-Honey Biscuit Mix* and ¼ cup *sugar.* Mix 1 beaten *egg* and 1¼ cups *milk;* add all at once to dry ingredients. Stir just till moistened. Fill greased 2½-inch muffin pans ⅔ full. Bake in 400° oven for 20 to 25 minutes. Makes 12 muffins.

INDEX

For timesaving tips, refer to pages 8, 10, 21, 41, 46, 51, 52, 55, 59, 66, 74, 85, 90, 91, and 92.